CREATURA - 4

70 drawings by Joan Worth

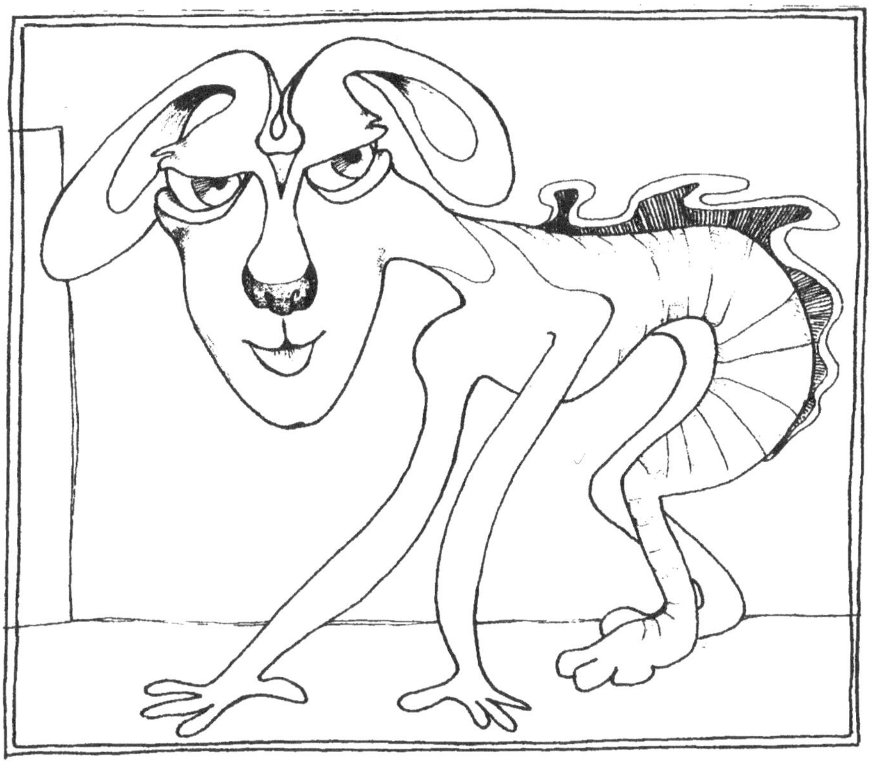

De Pere, Wisconsin
ISBN-13: 978-1984914170
ISBN-10: 1984914170

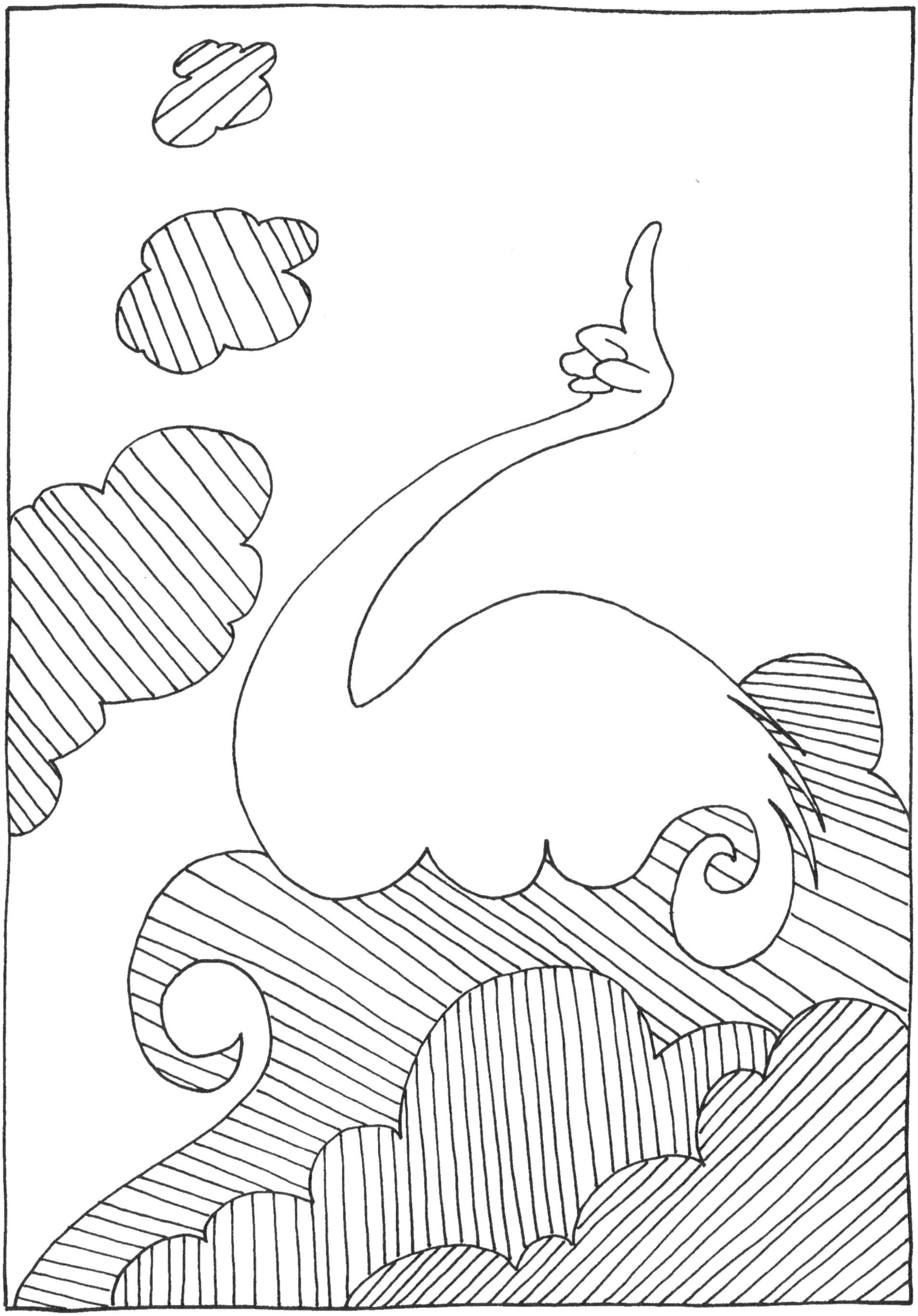

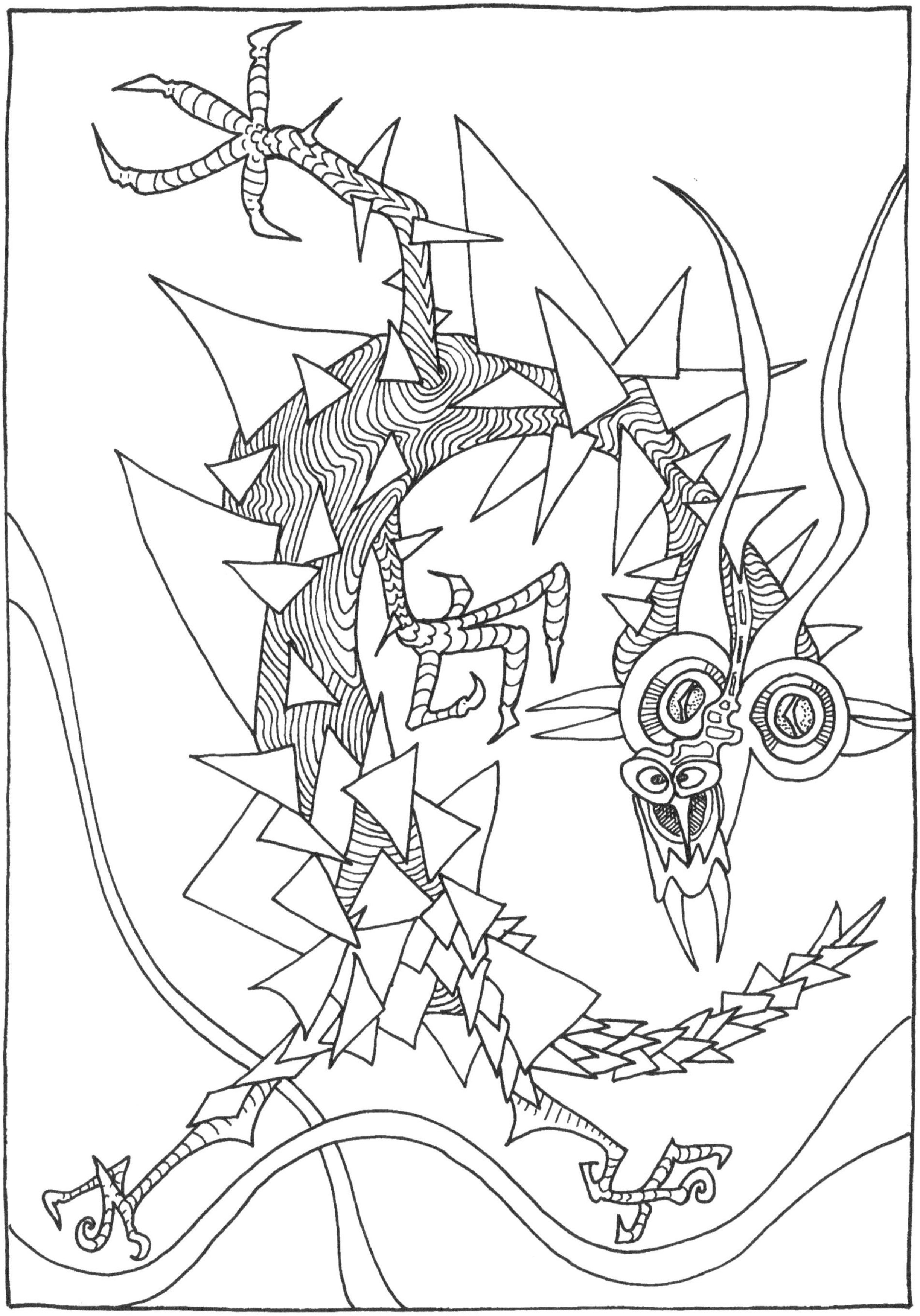

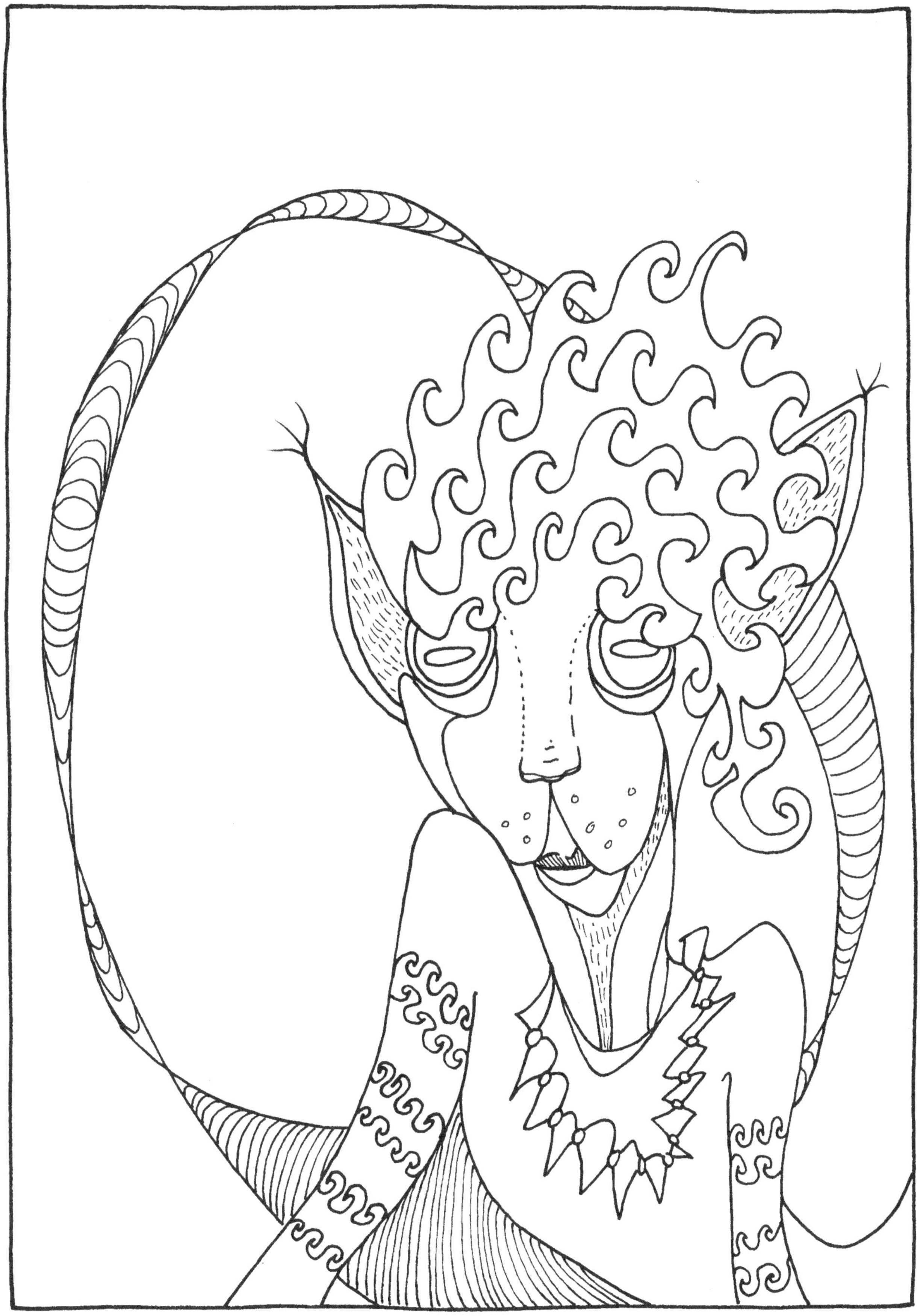

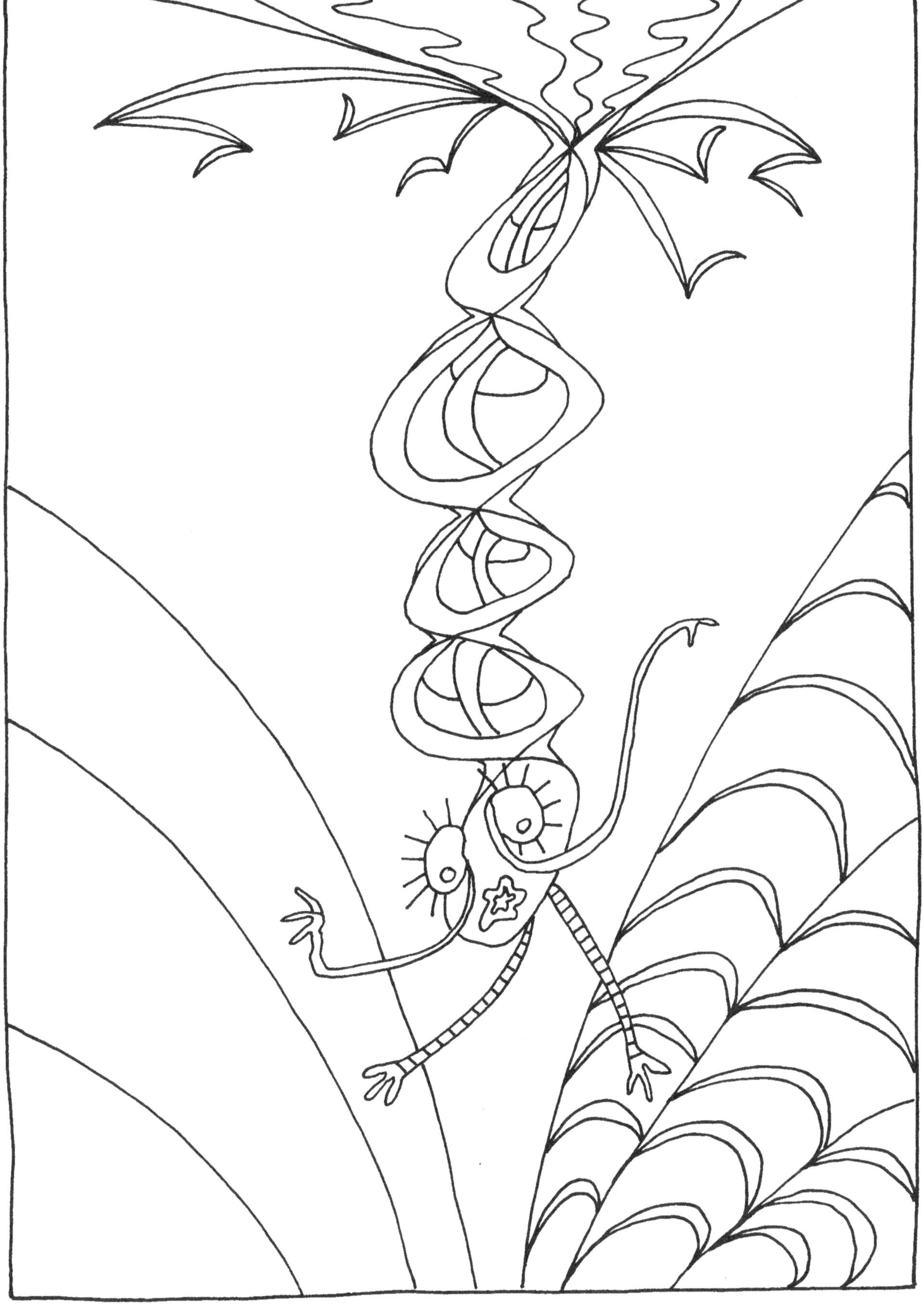

CREATURA #4

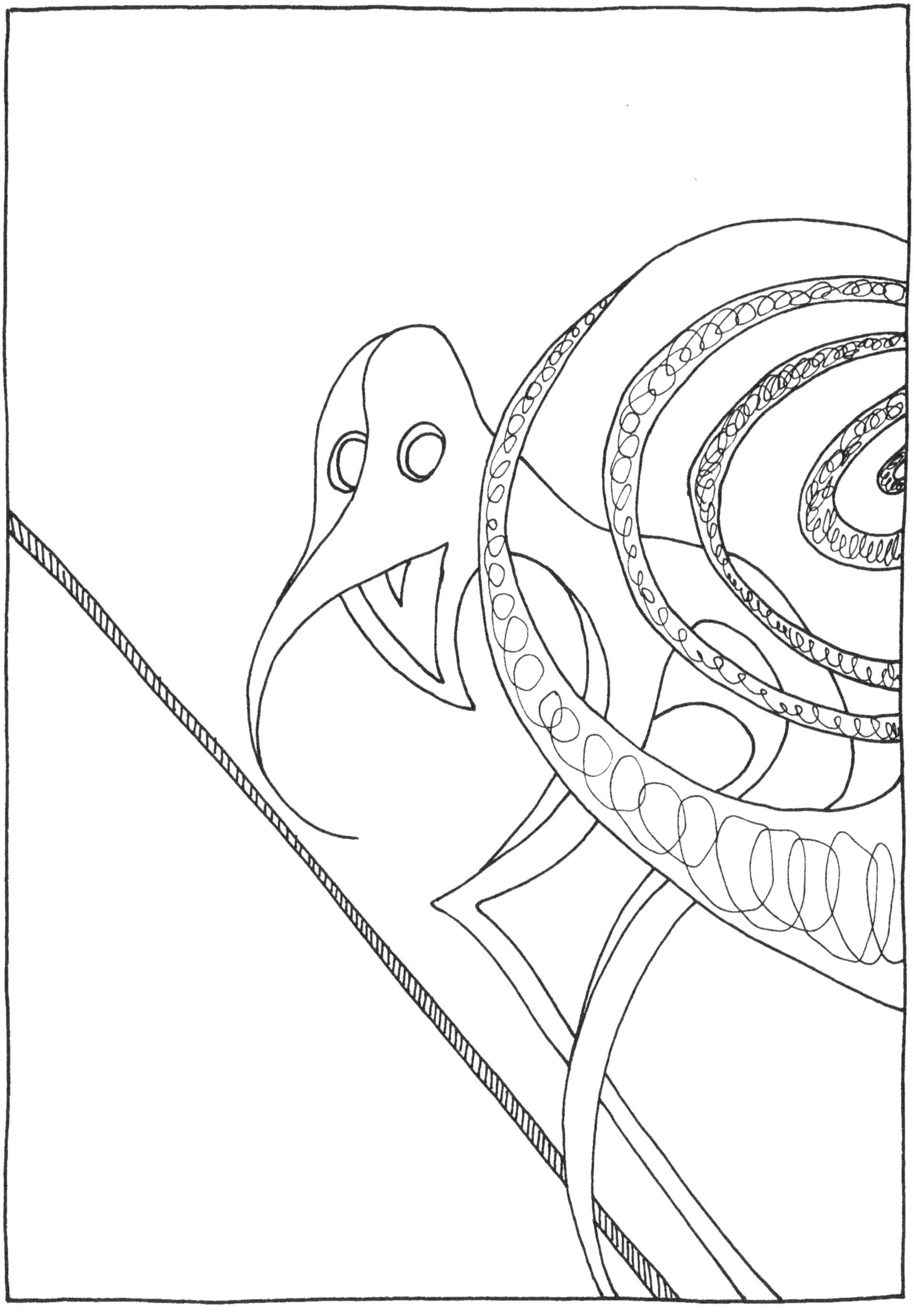

CREATURA #4

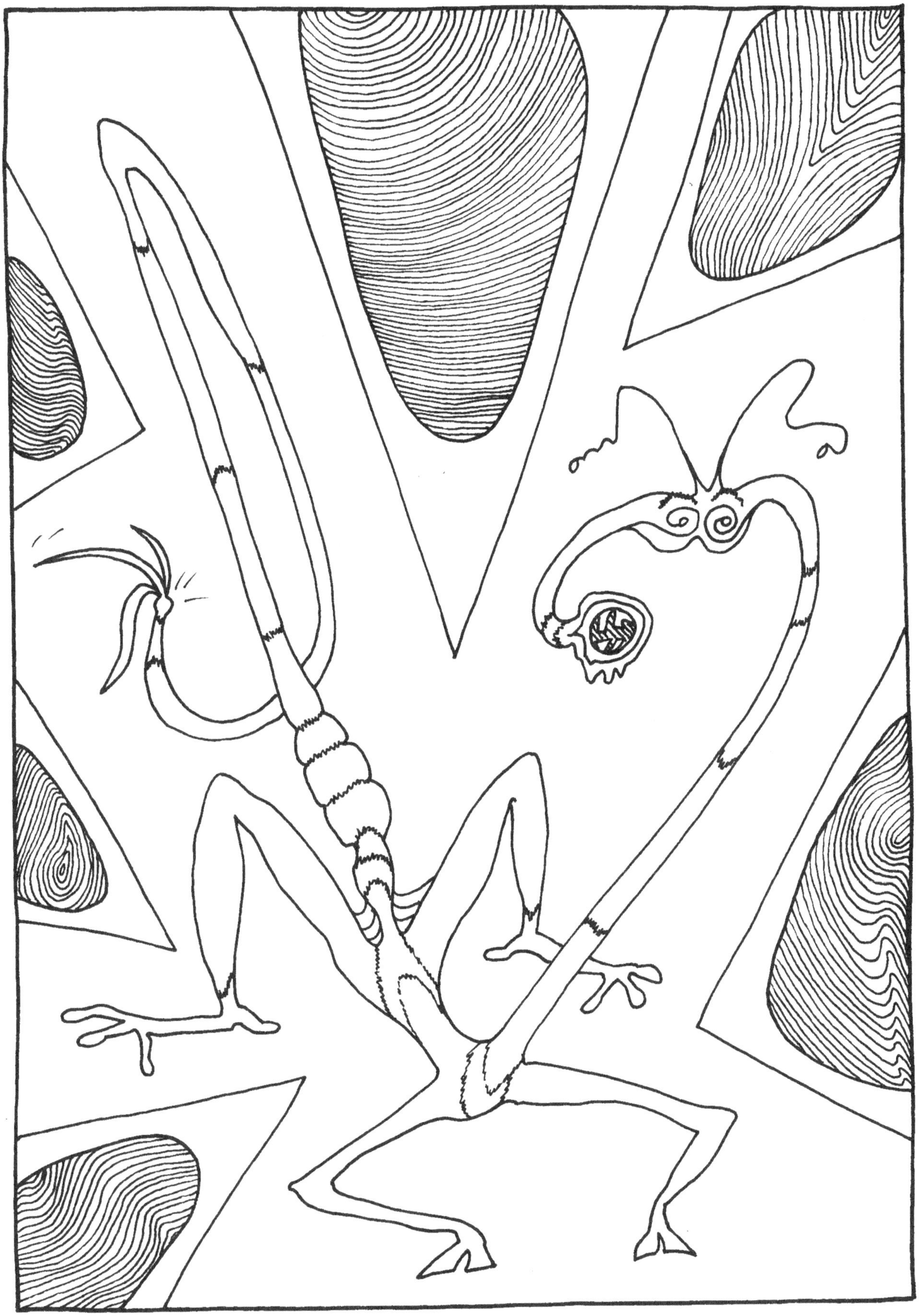

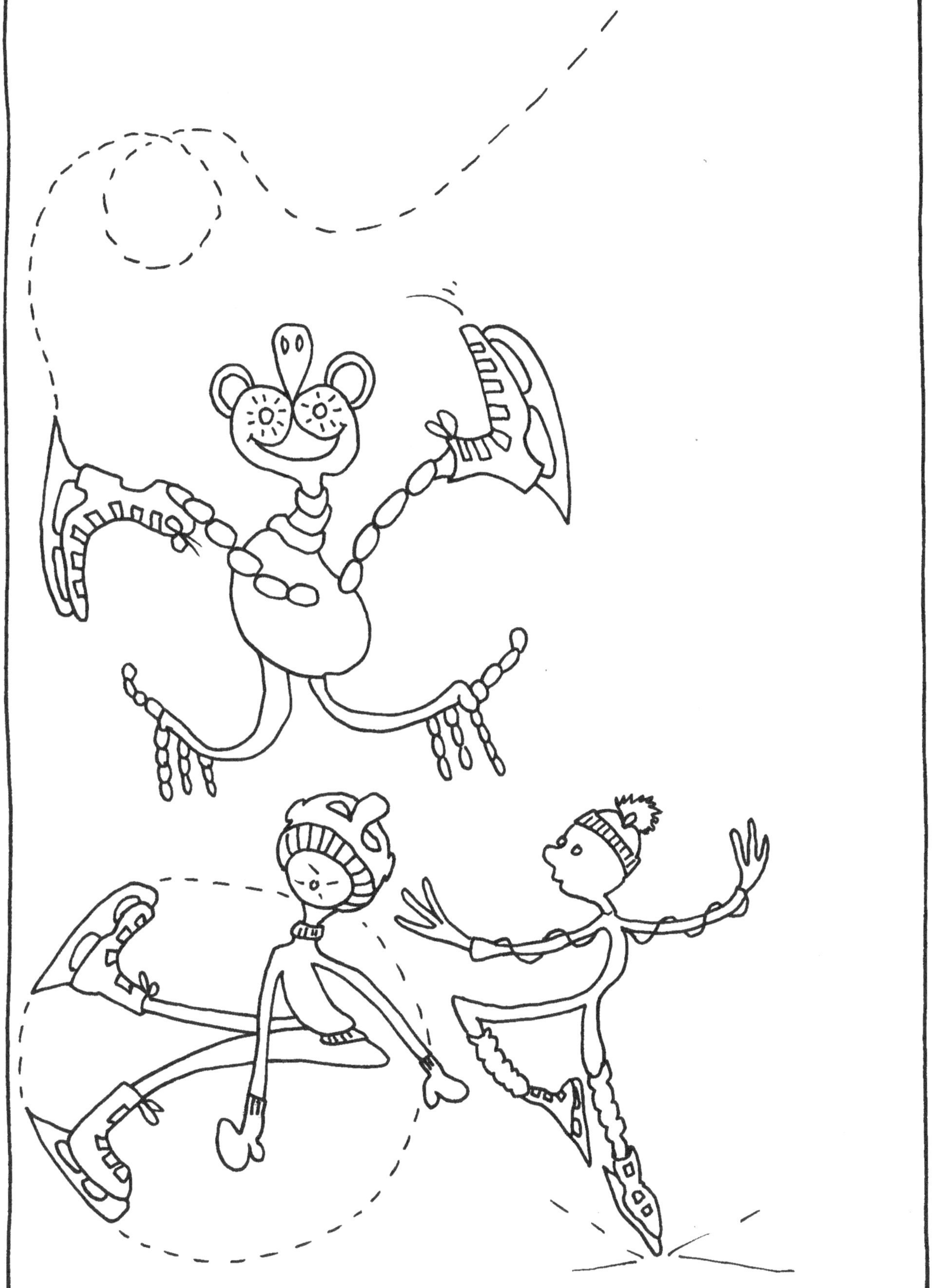

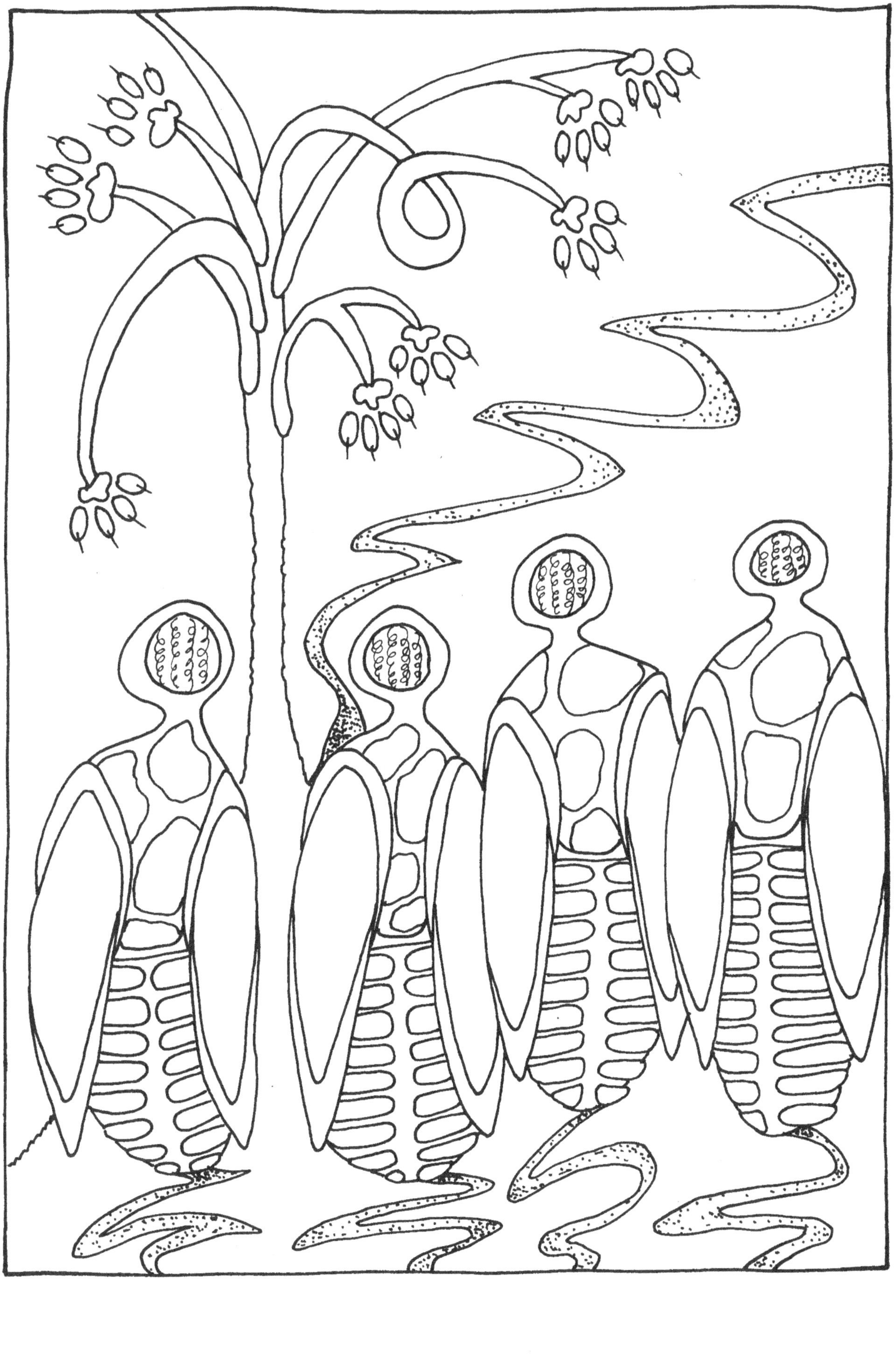

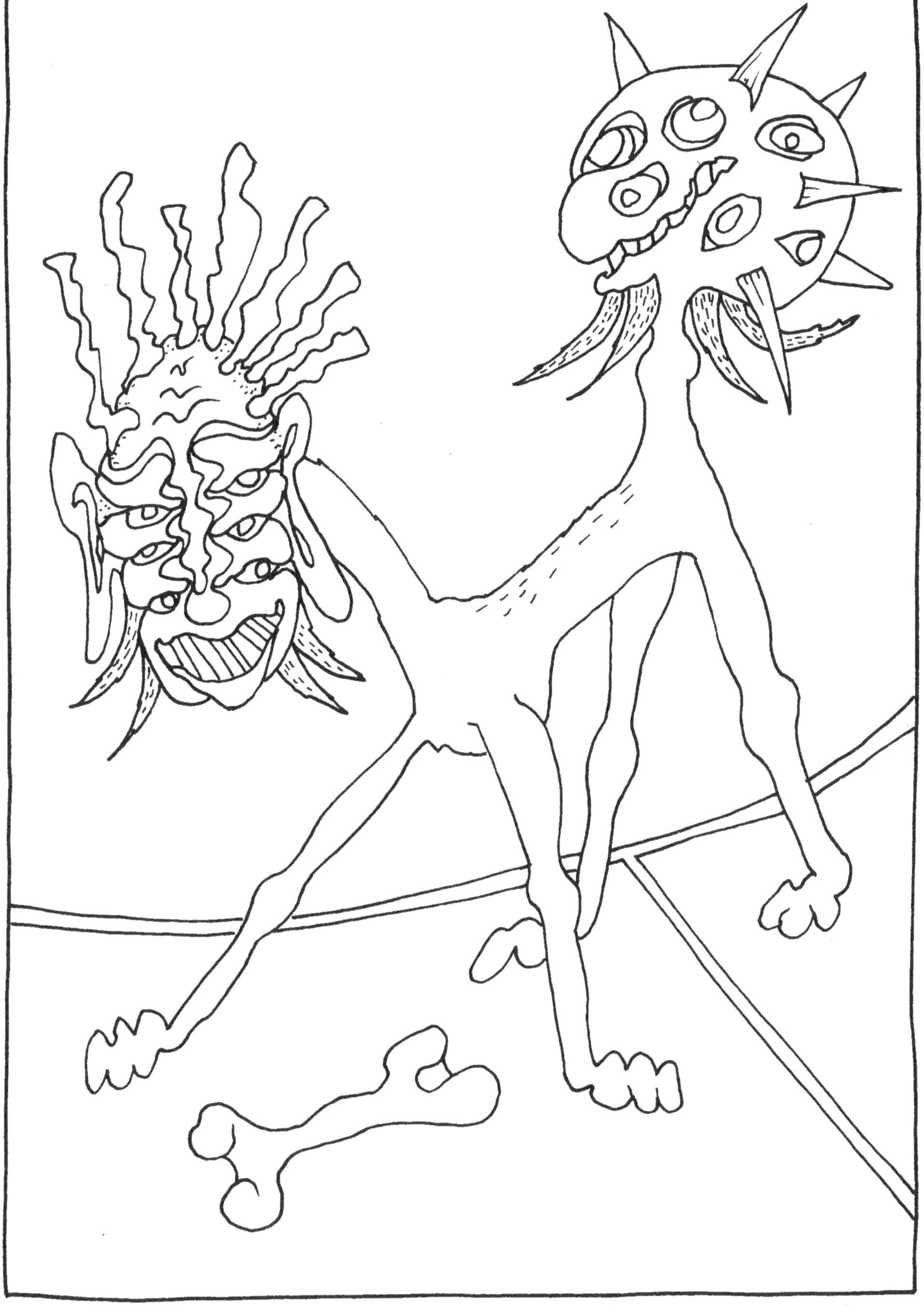

CREATURA #4 ©2018 Joan Worth

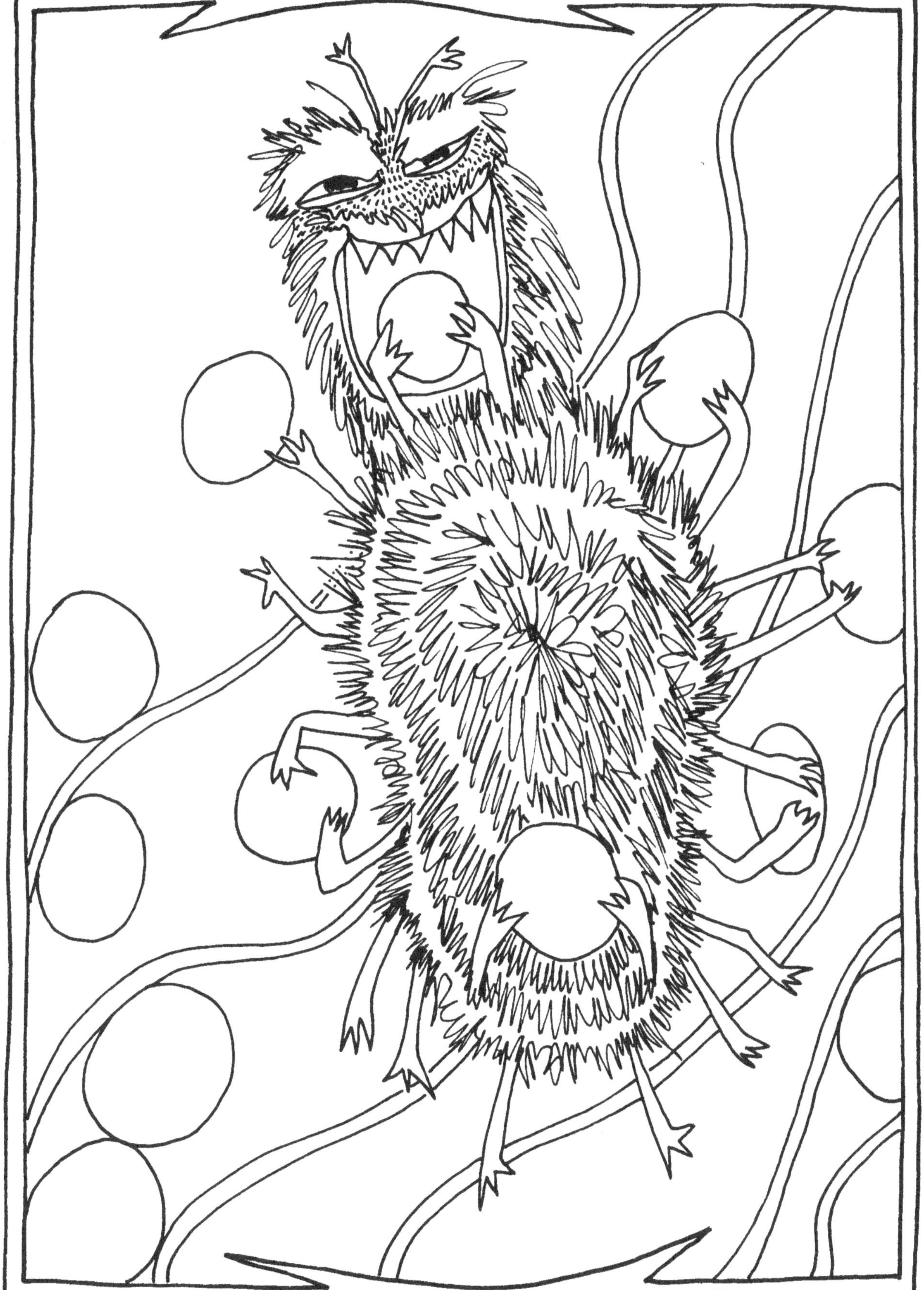

CREATURA #4

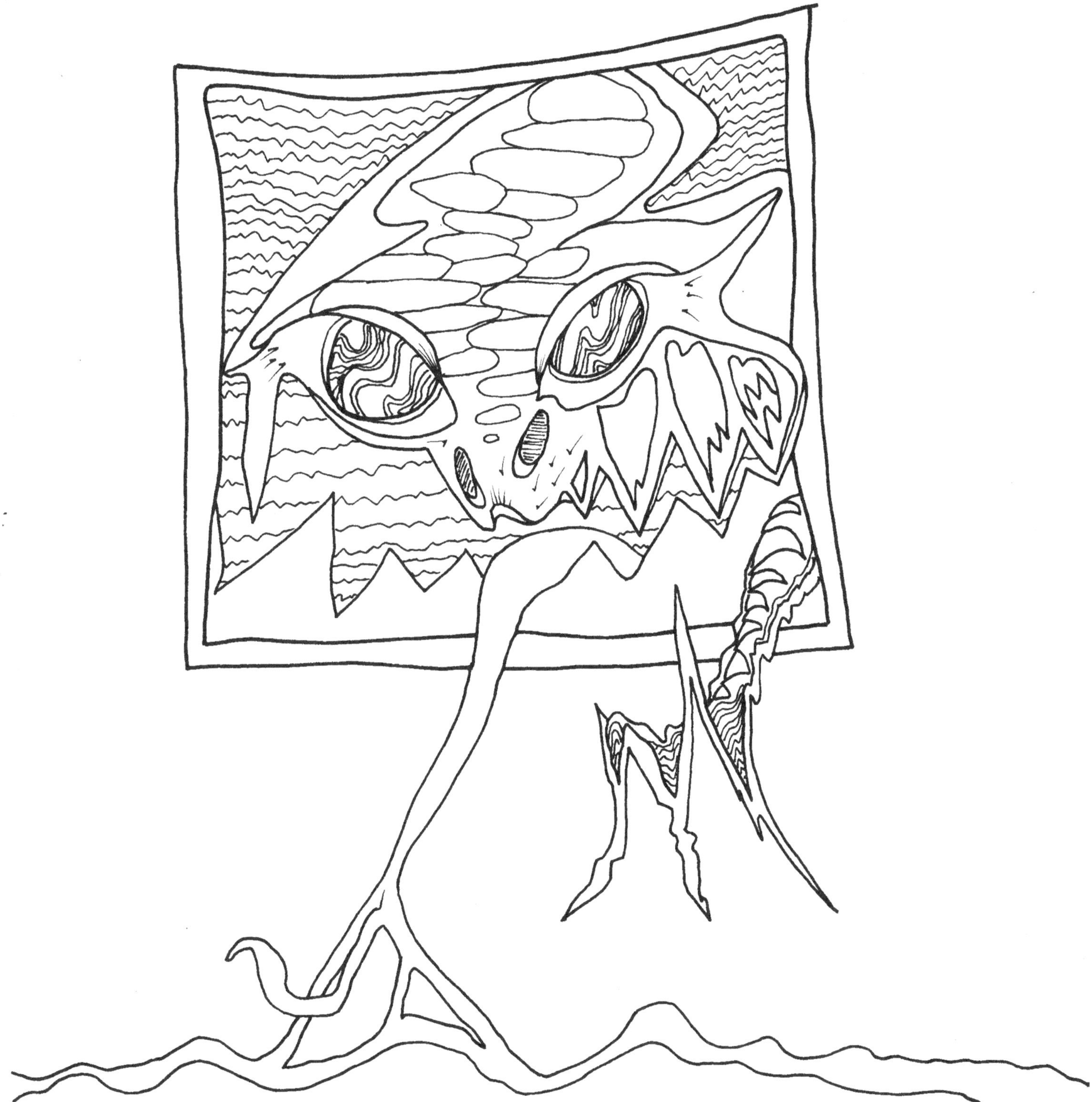

CREATURA #4

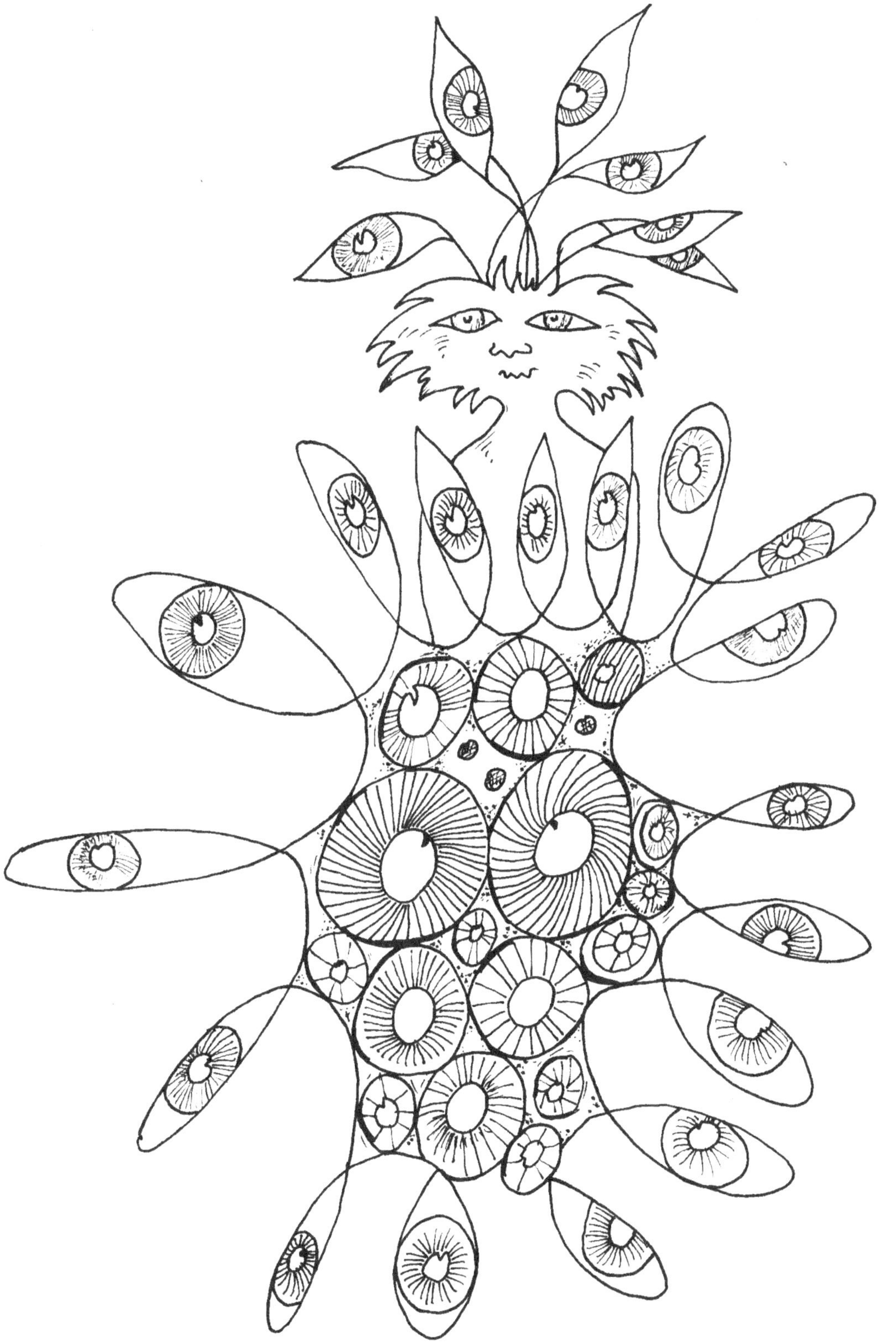

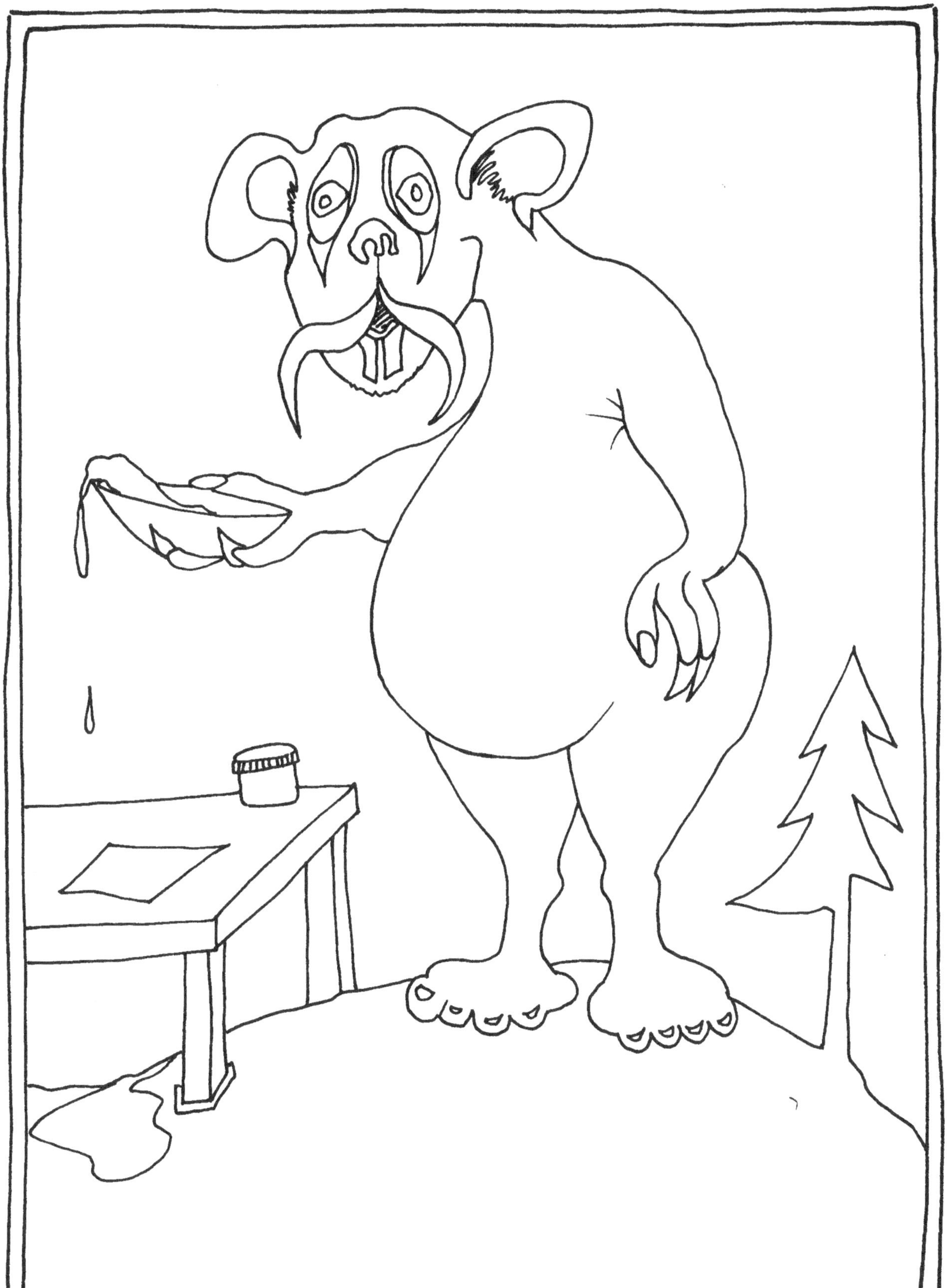

CREATURA #4 ©2018 Joan Worth

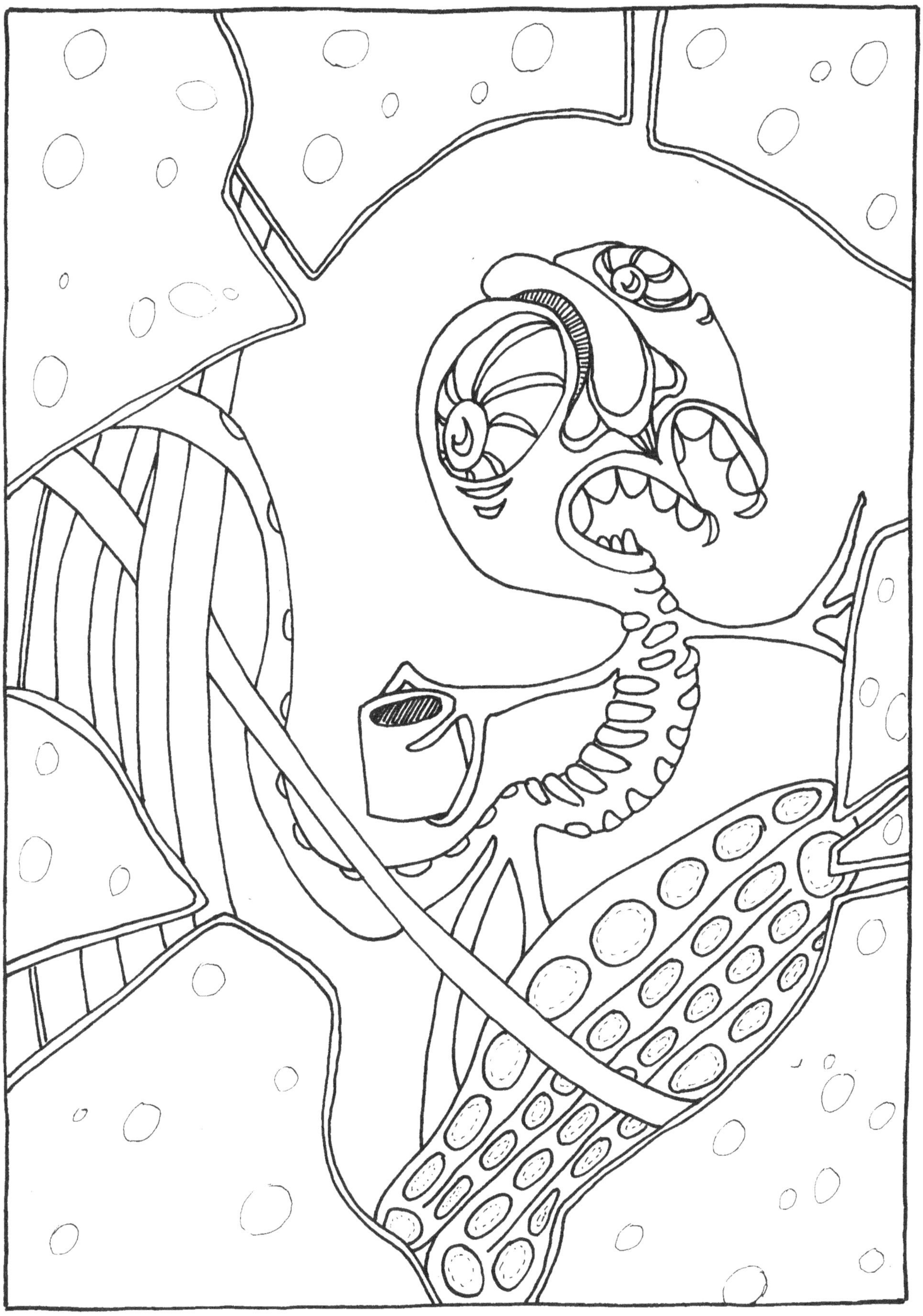

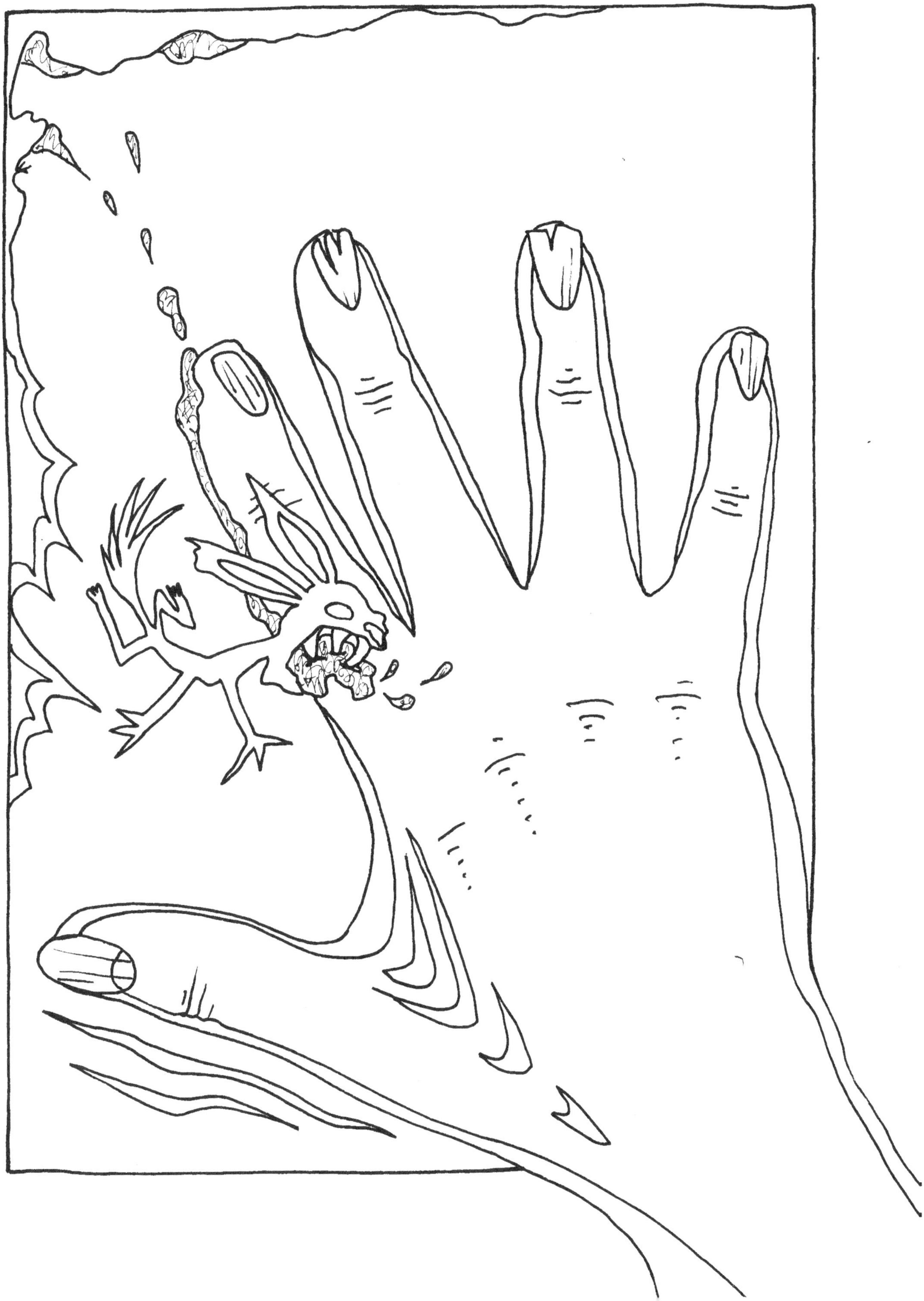

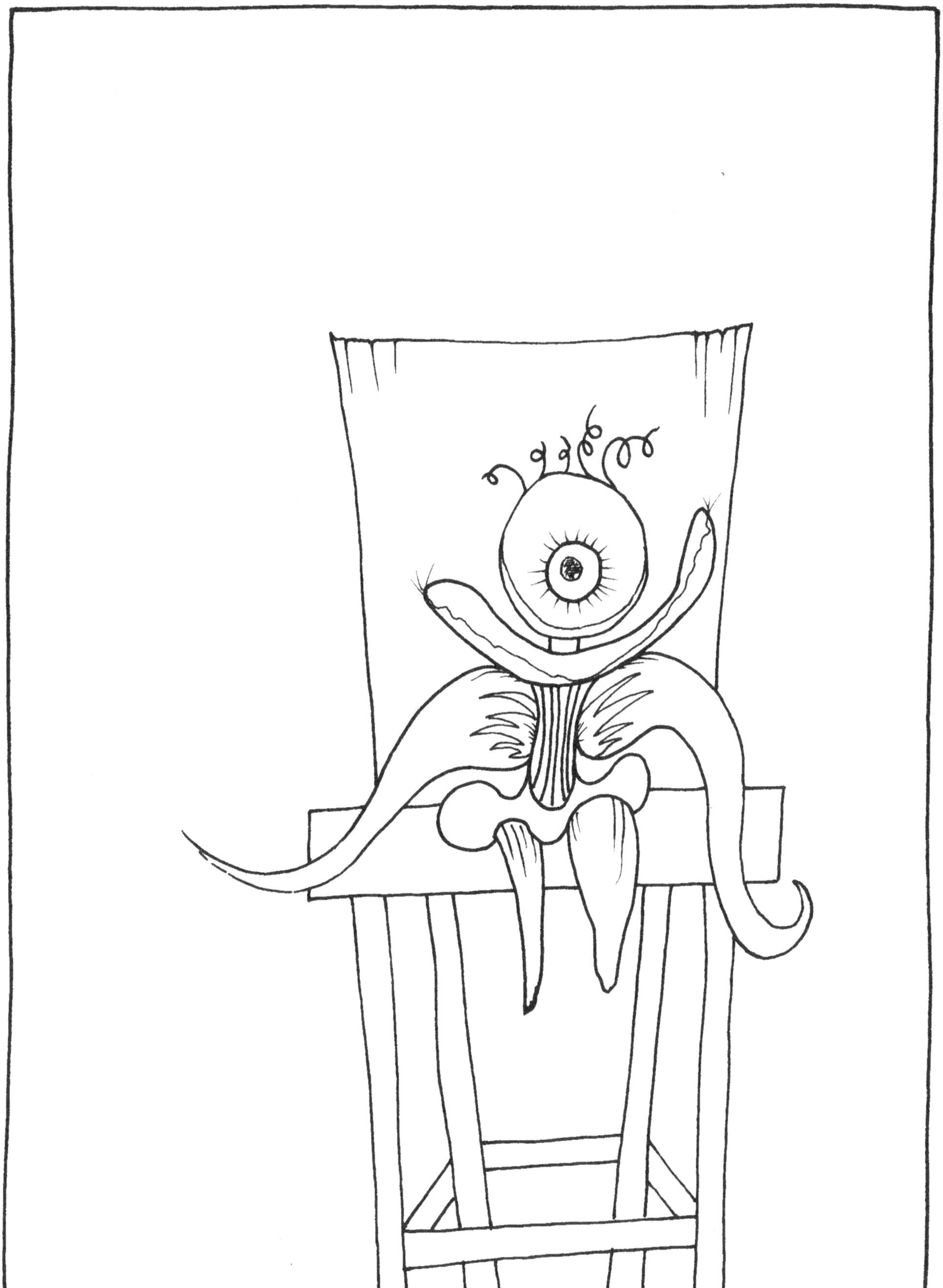

CREATURA #4

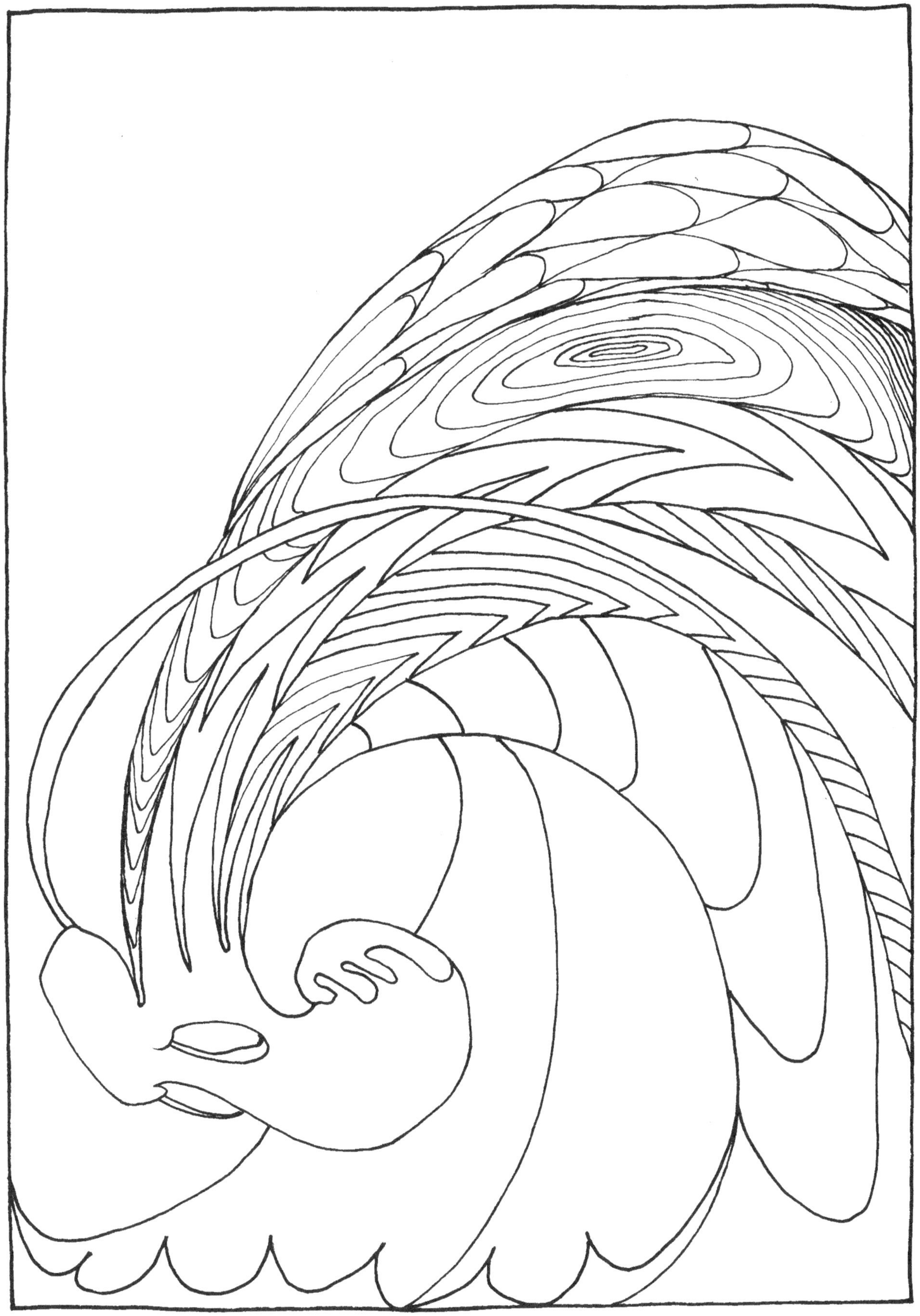

CREATURA #4

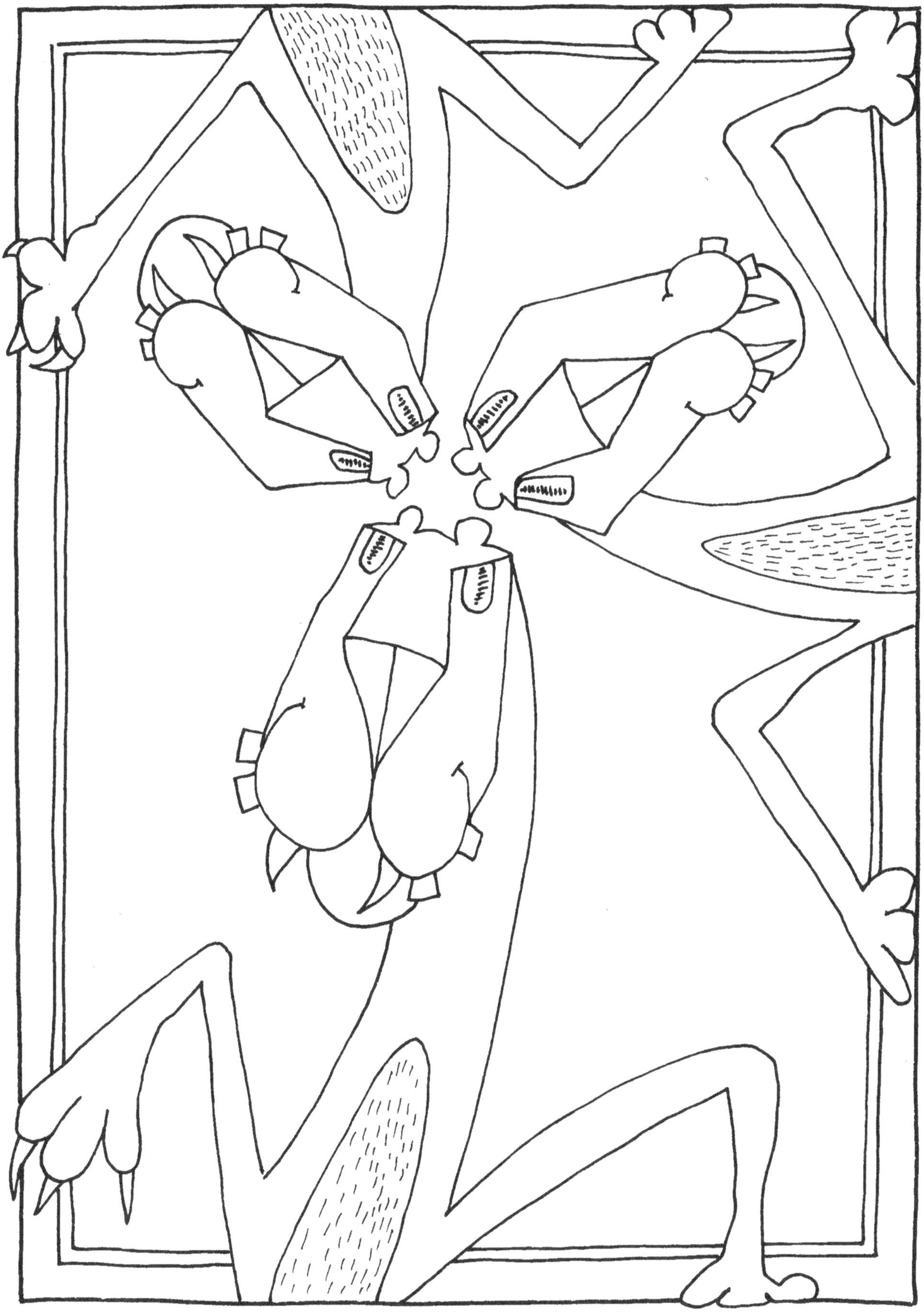

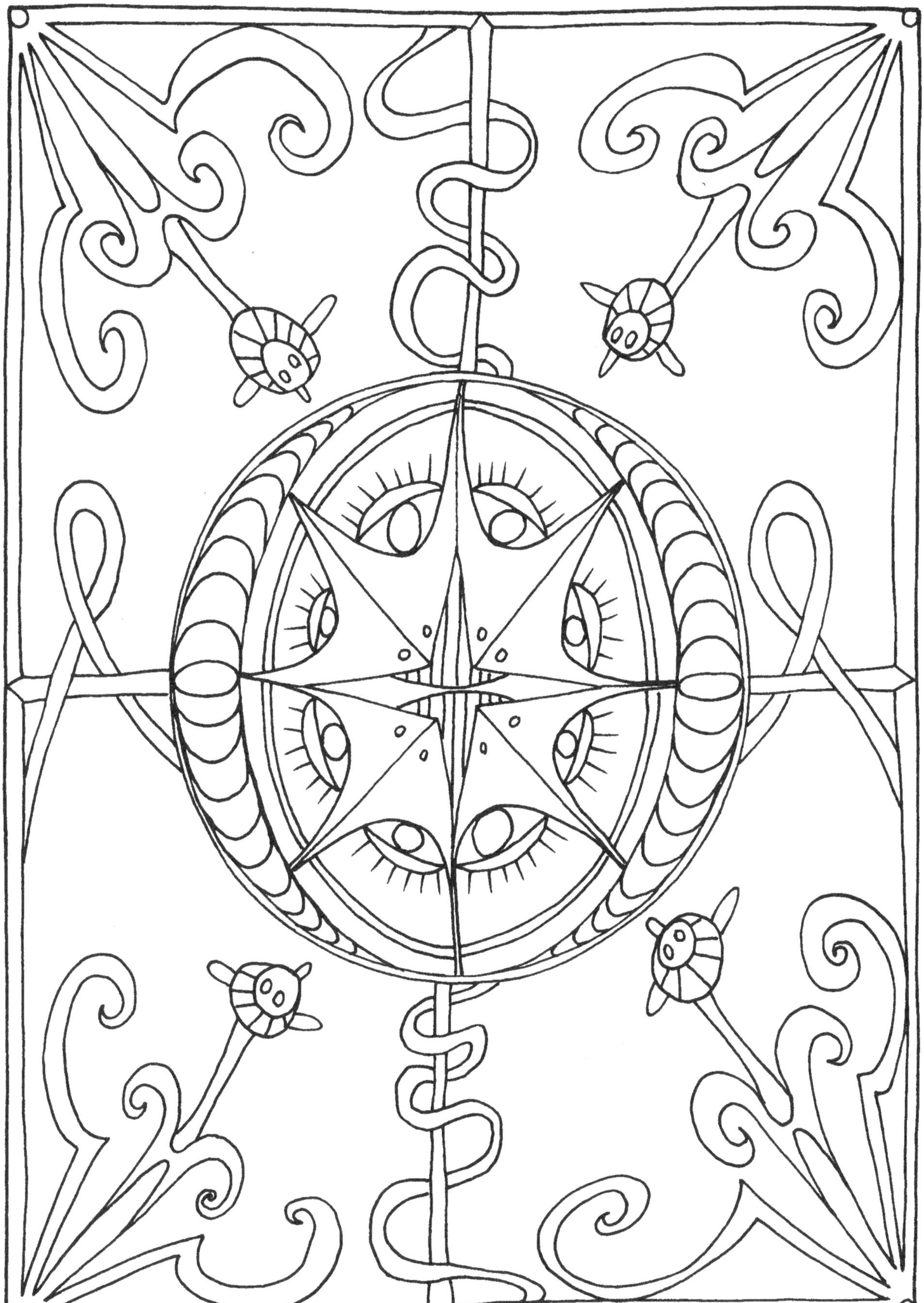

CREATURA #4 ©2018 Joan Worth

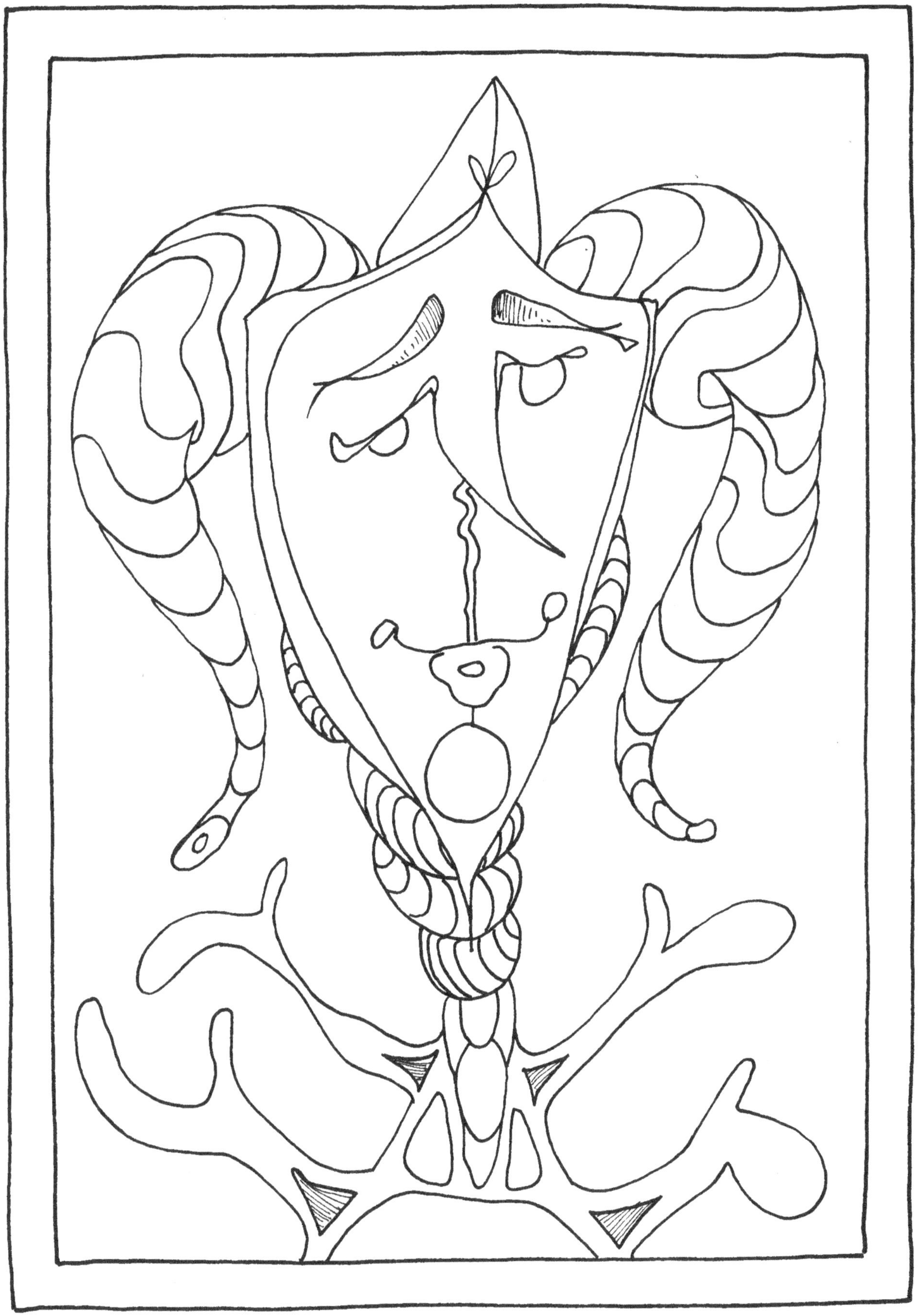

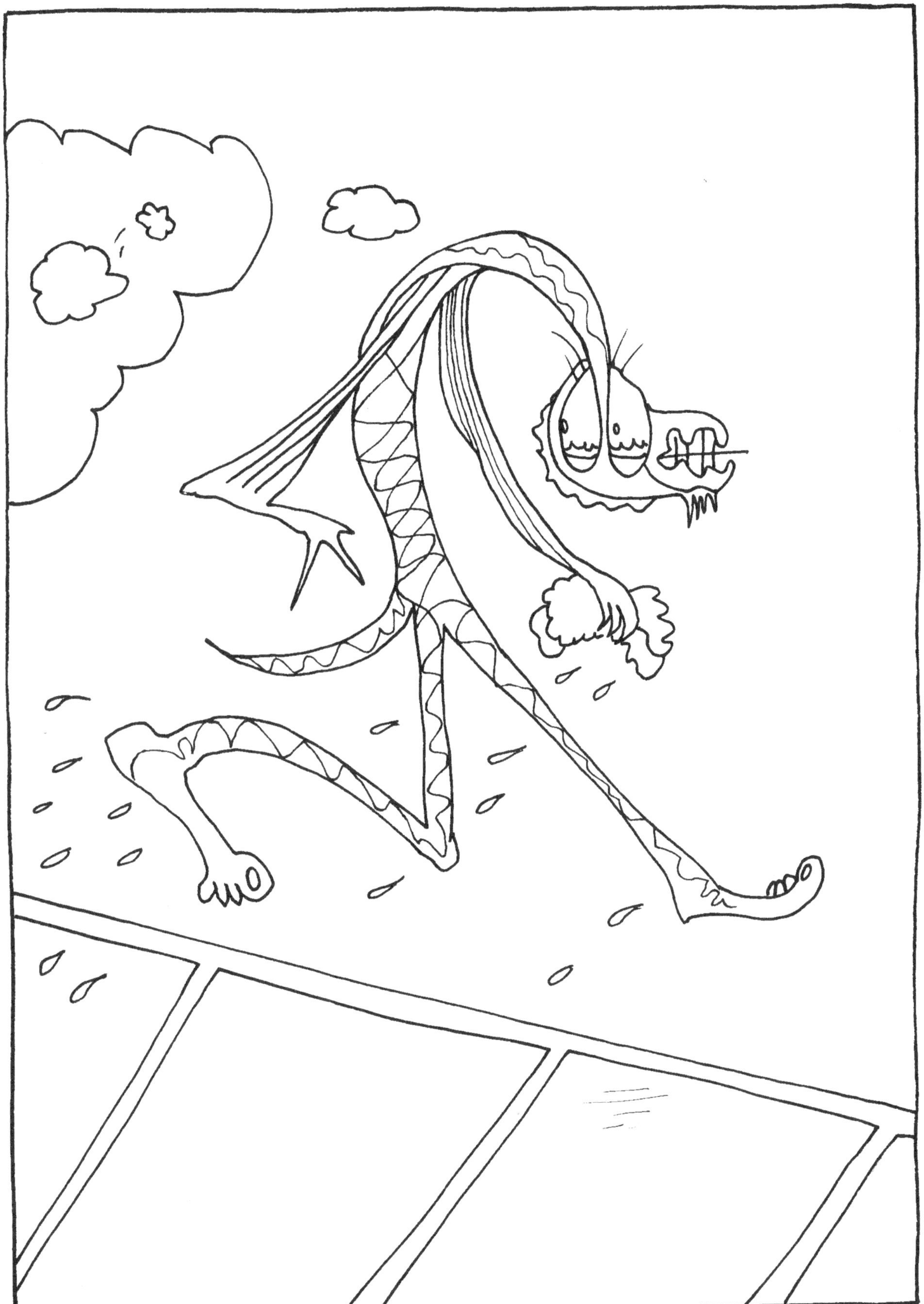

CREATURA #4

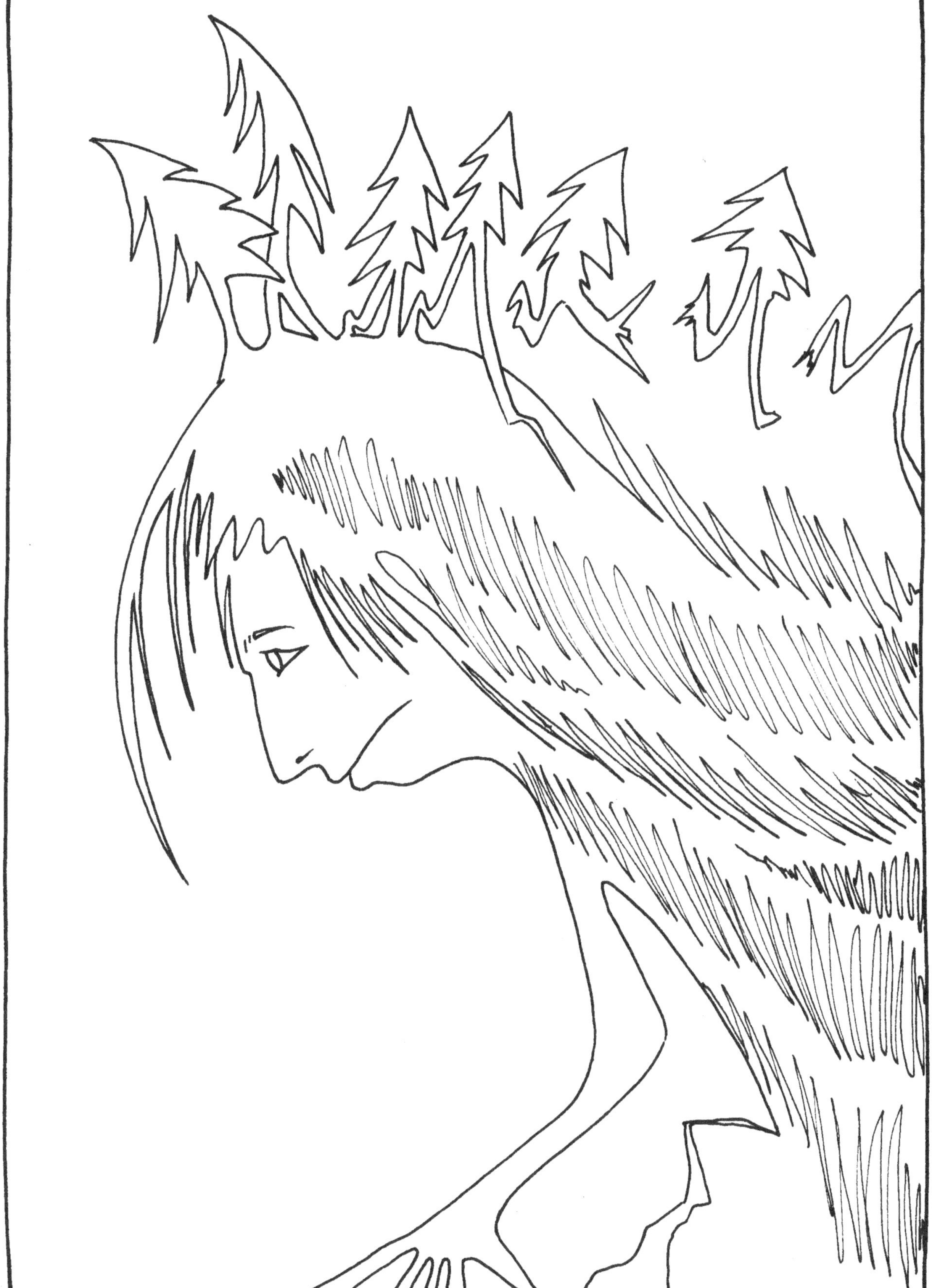

CREATURA #4 ©2018 Joan Worth

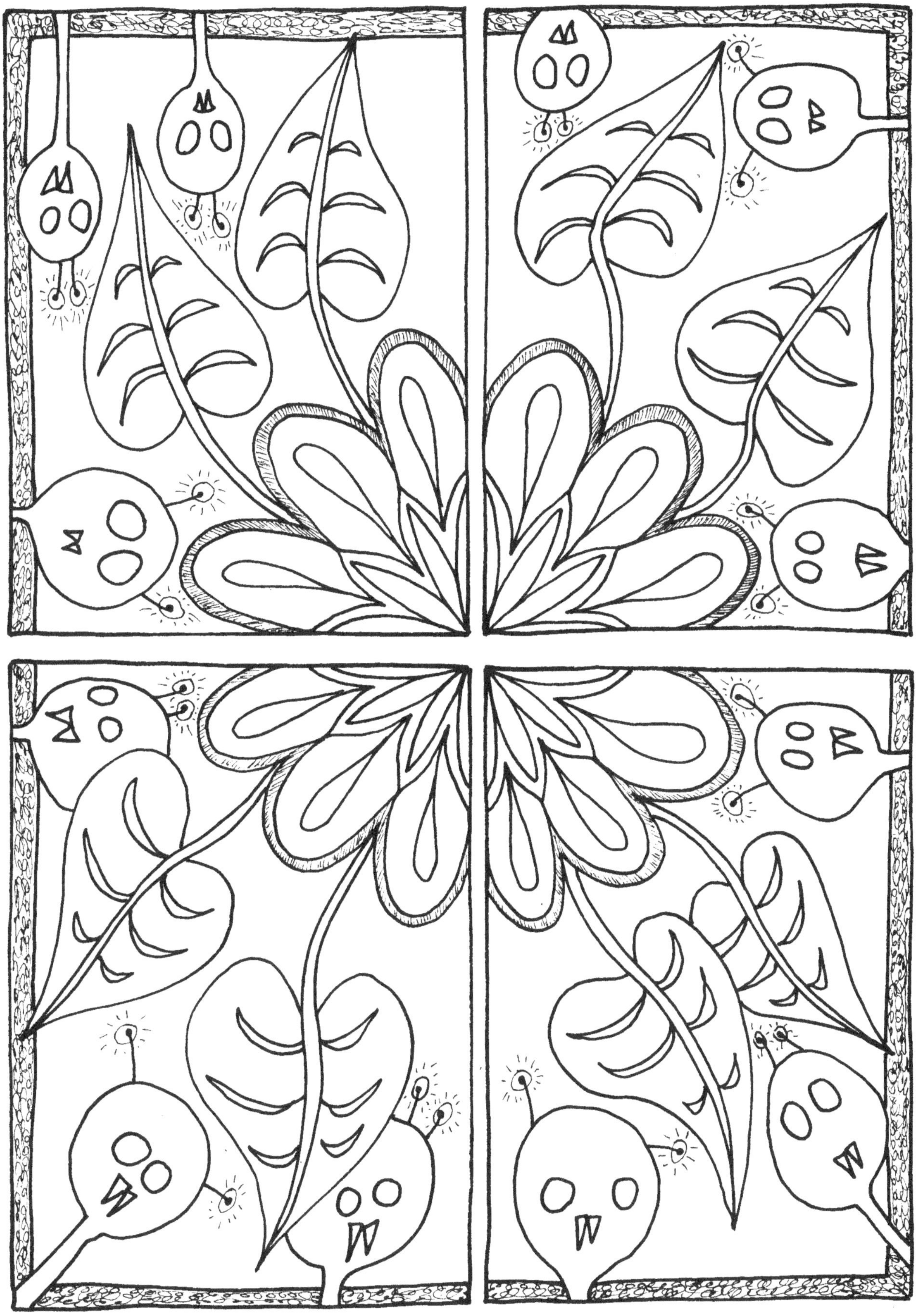

CREATURA #4 ©2018 Joan Worth

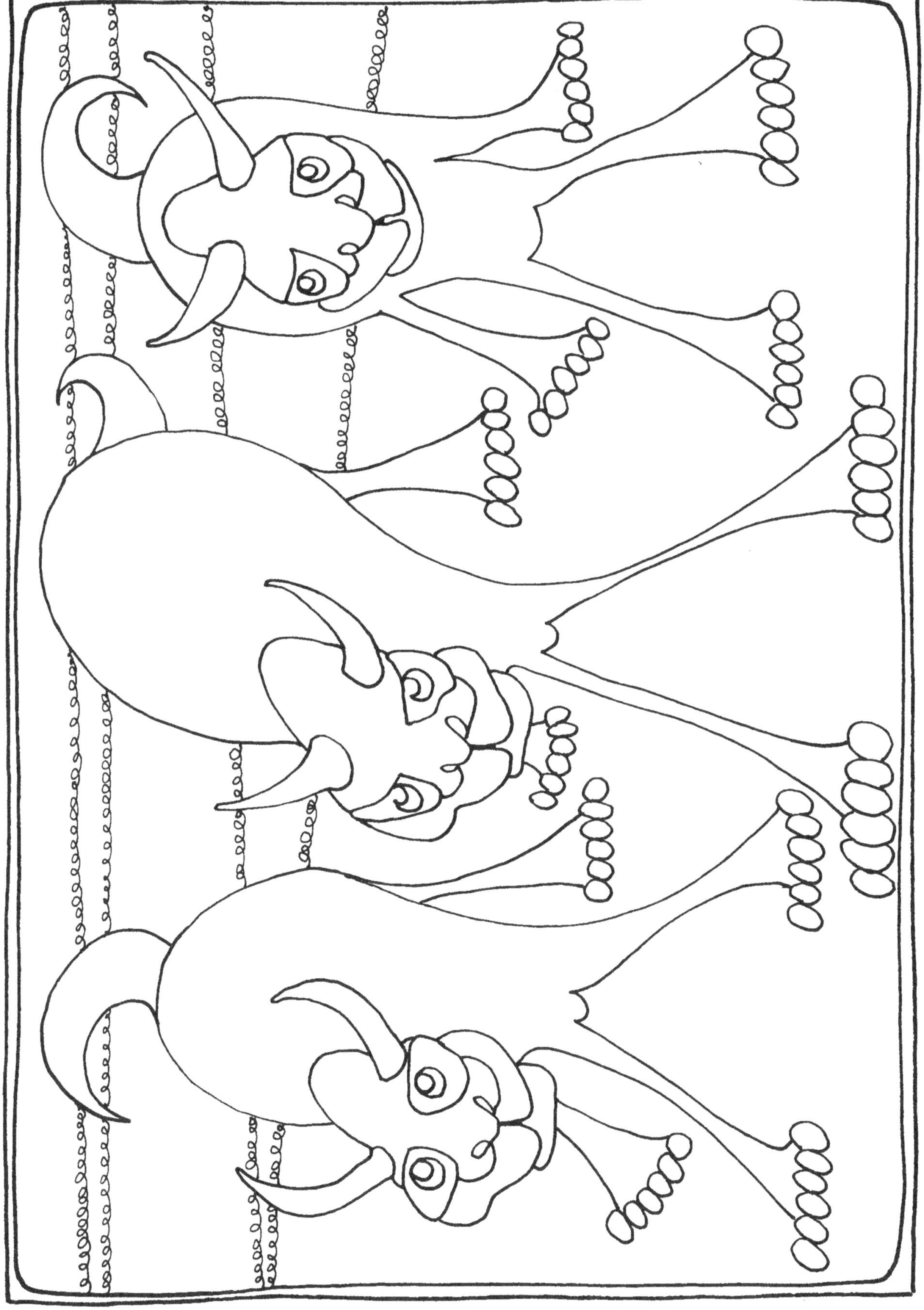

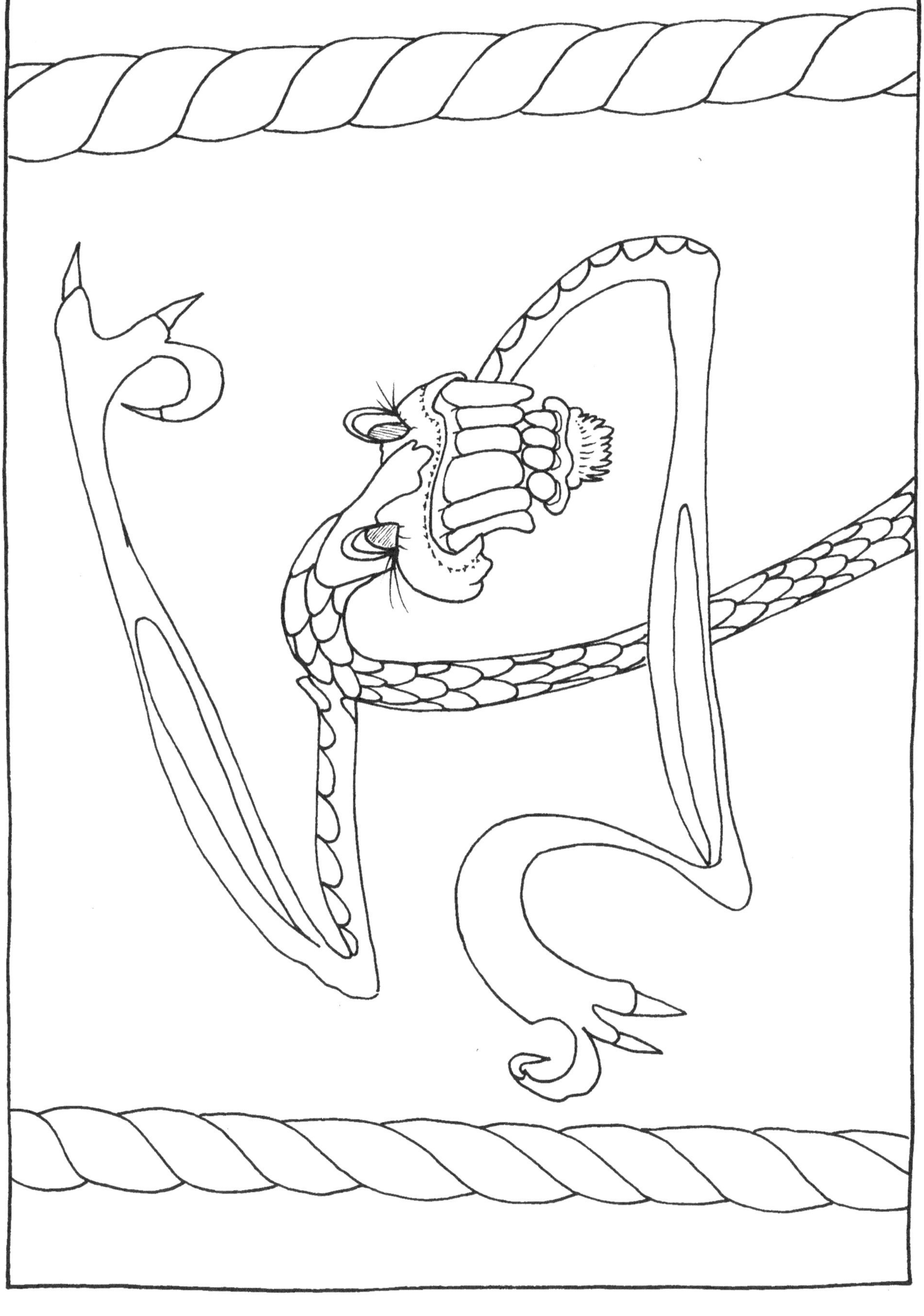

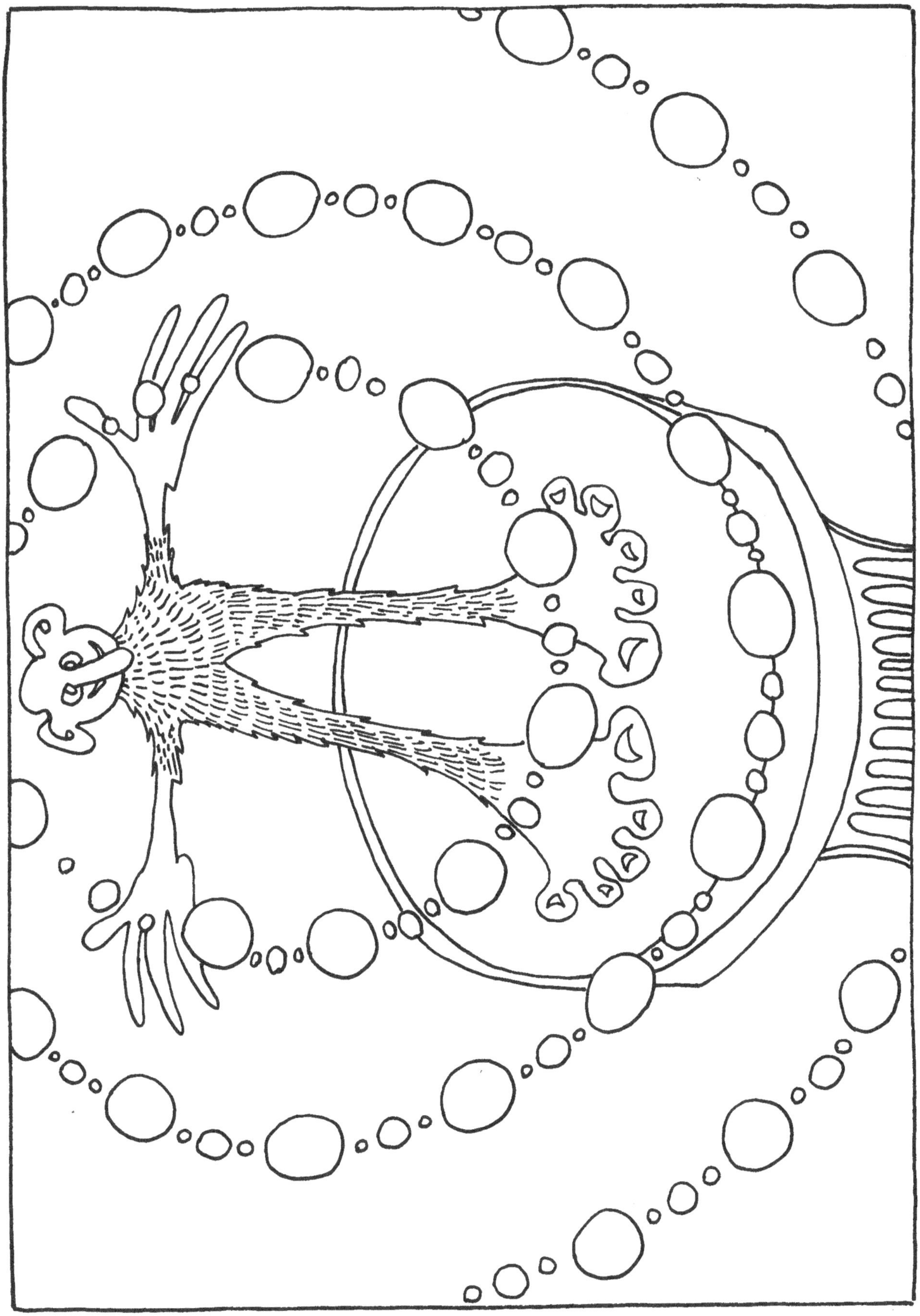

CREATURA #4

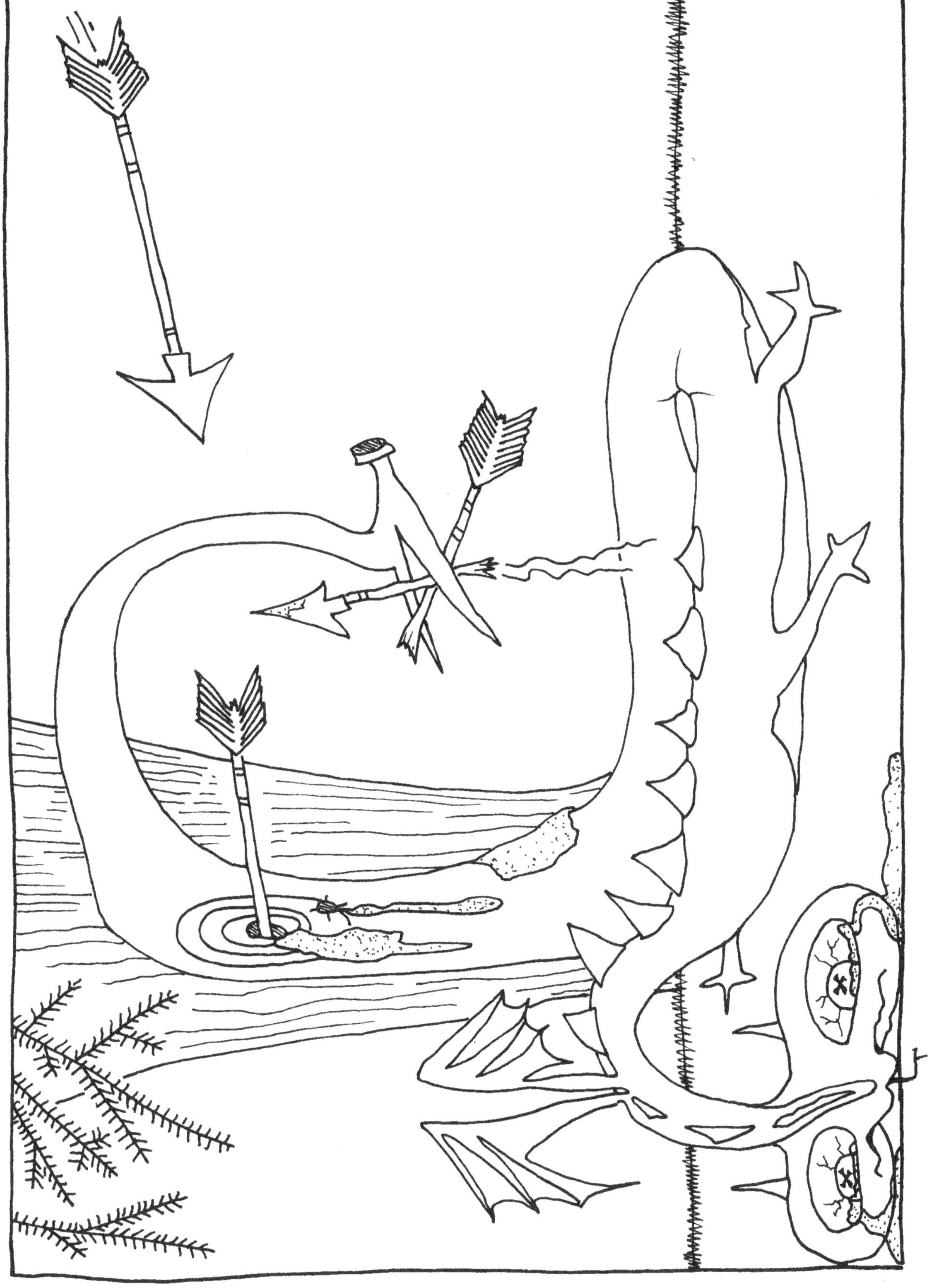

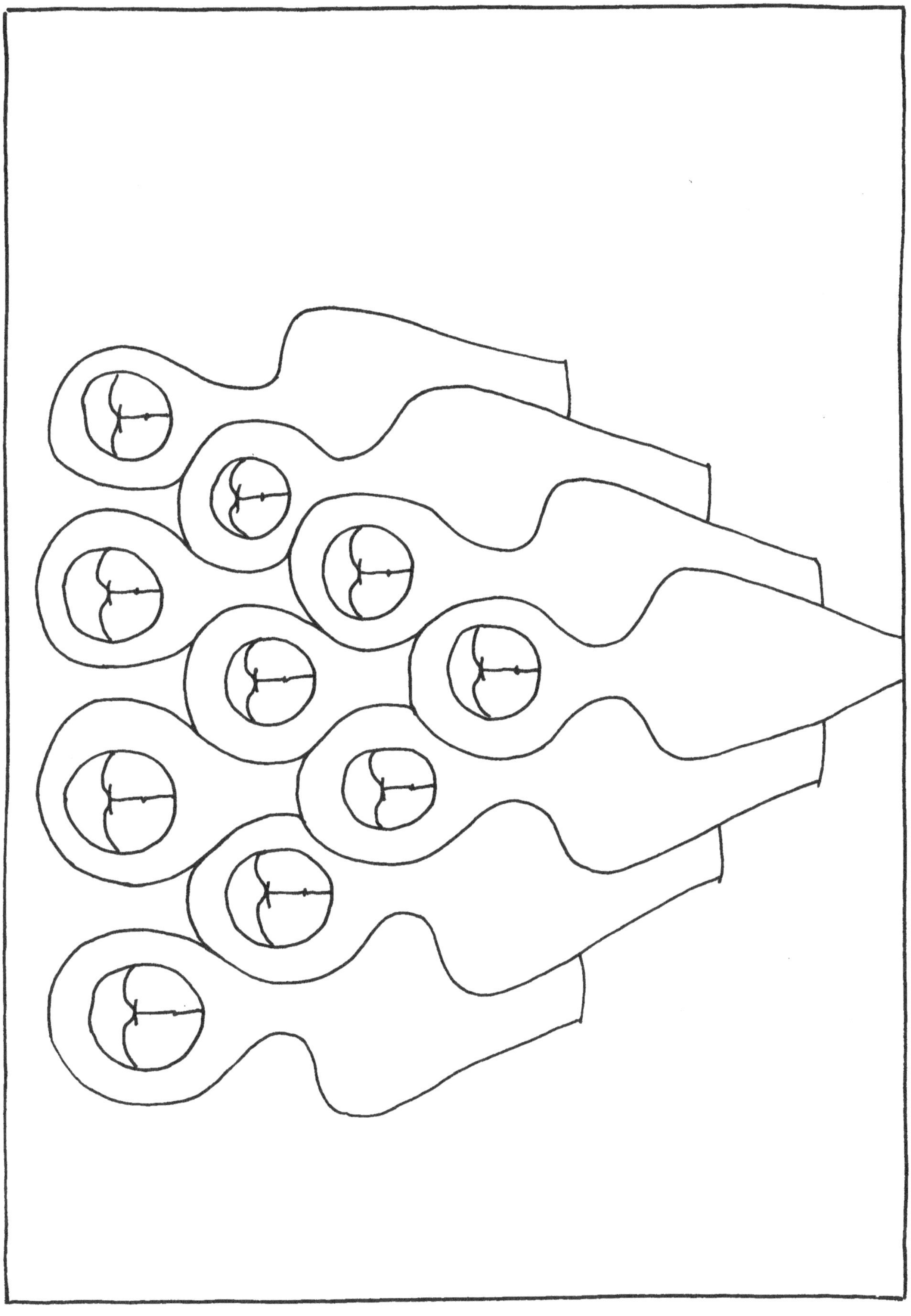

CREATURA #4 ©2018 Joan Worth

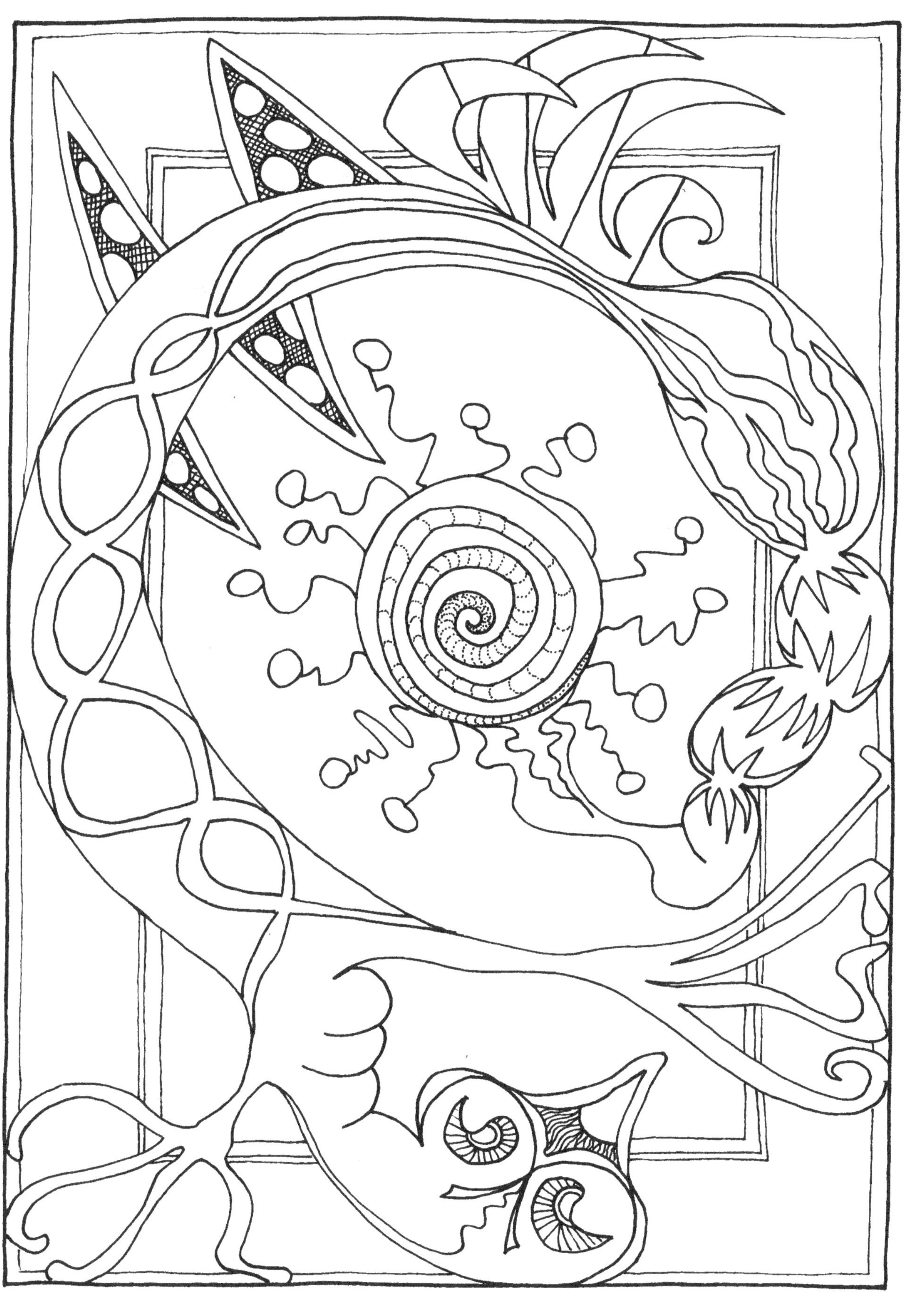

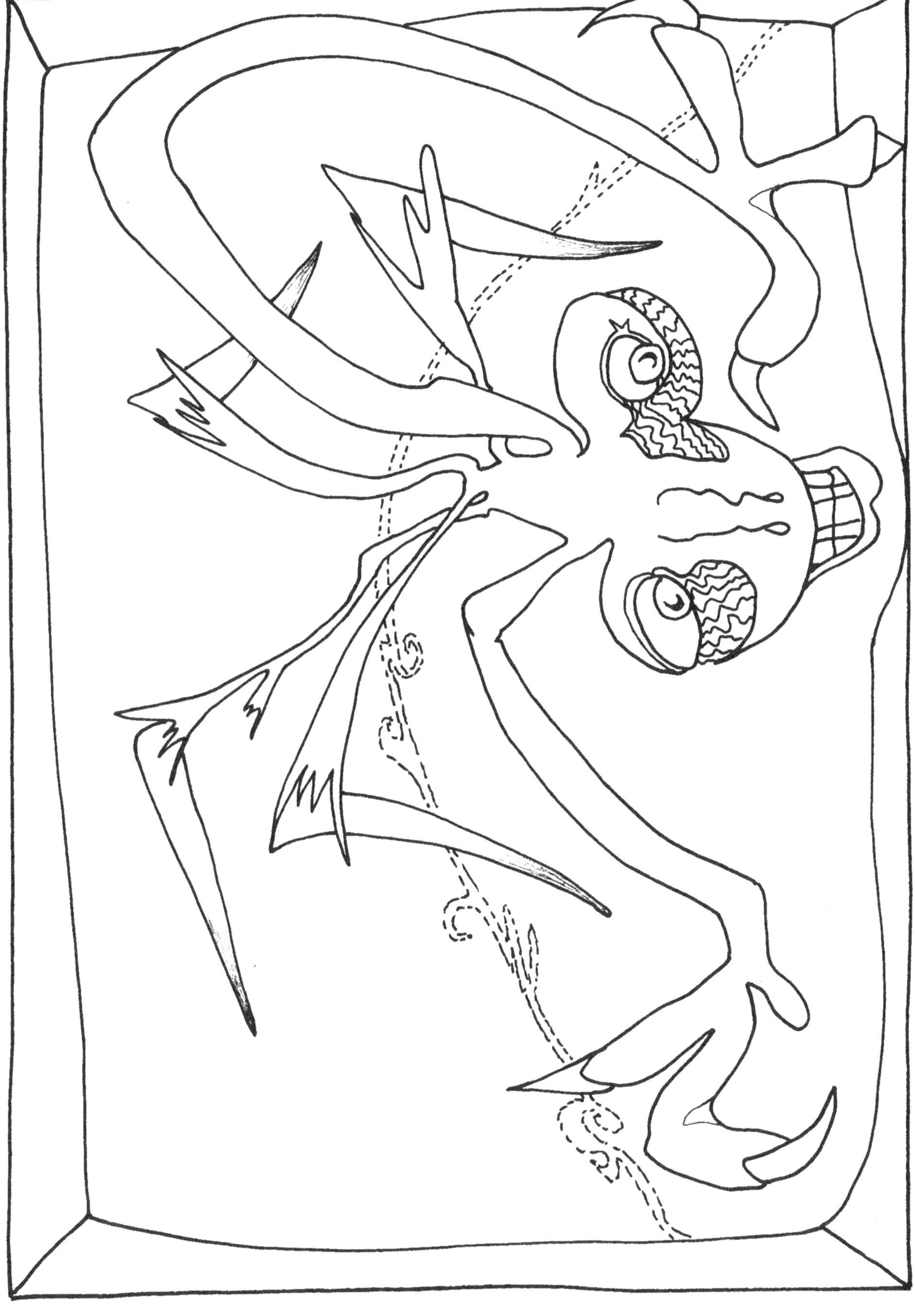

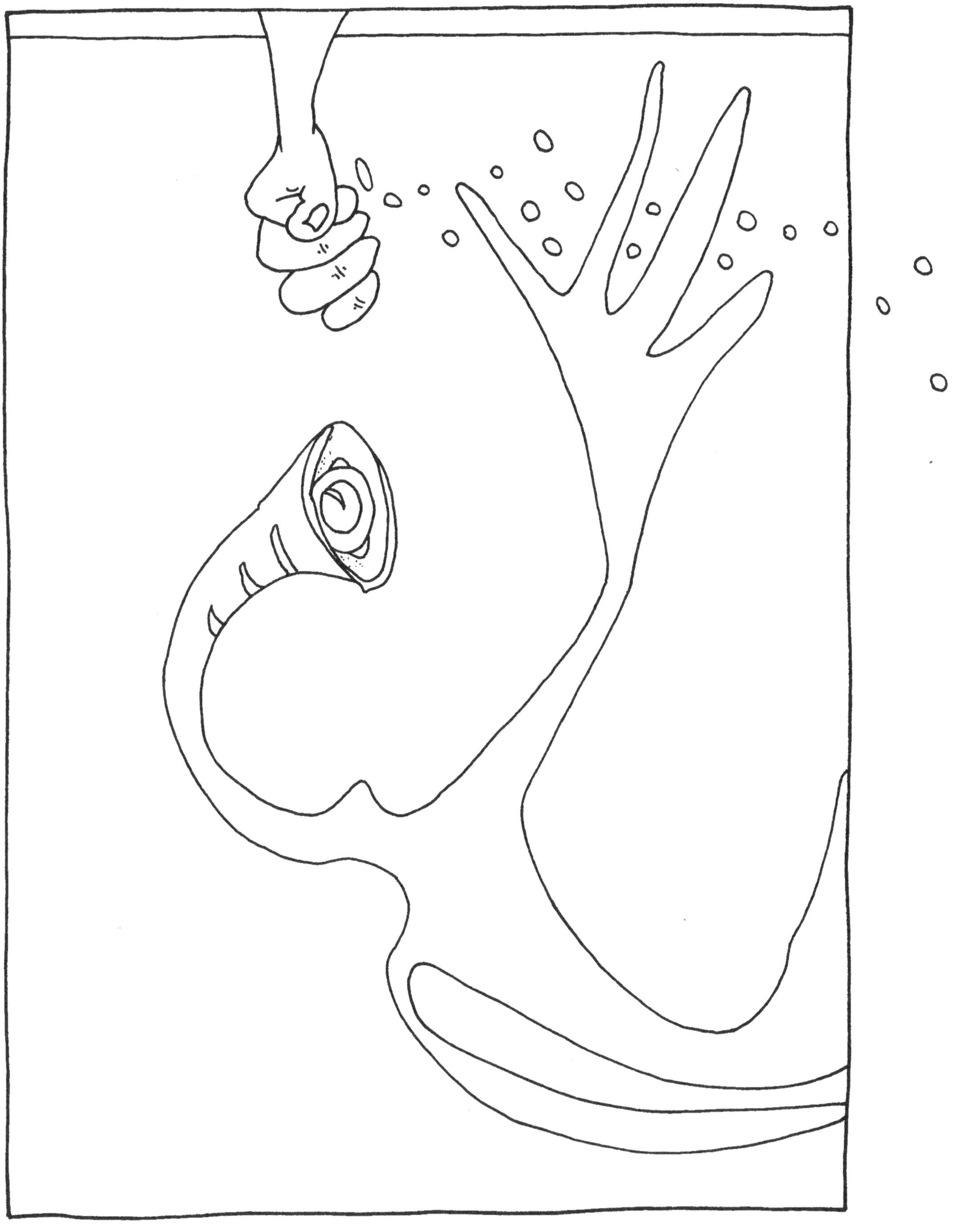

CREATURA #4

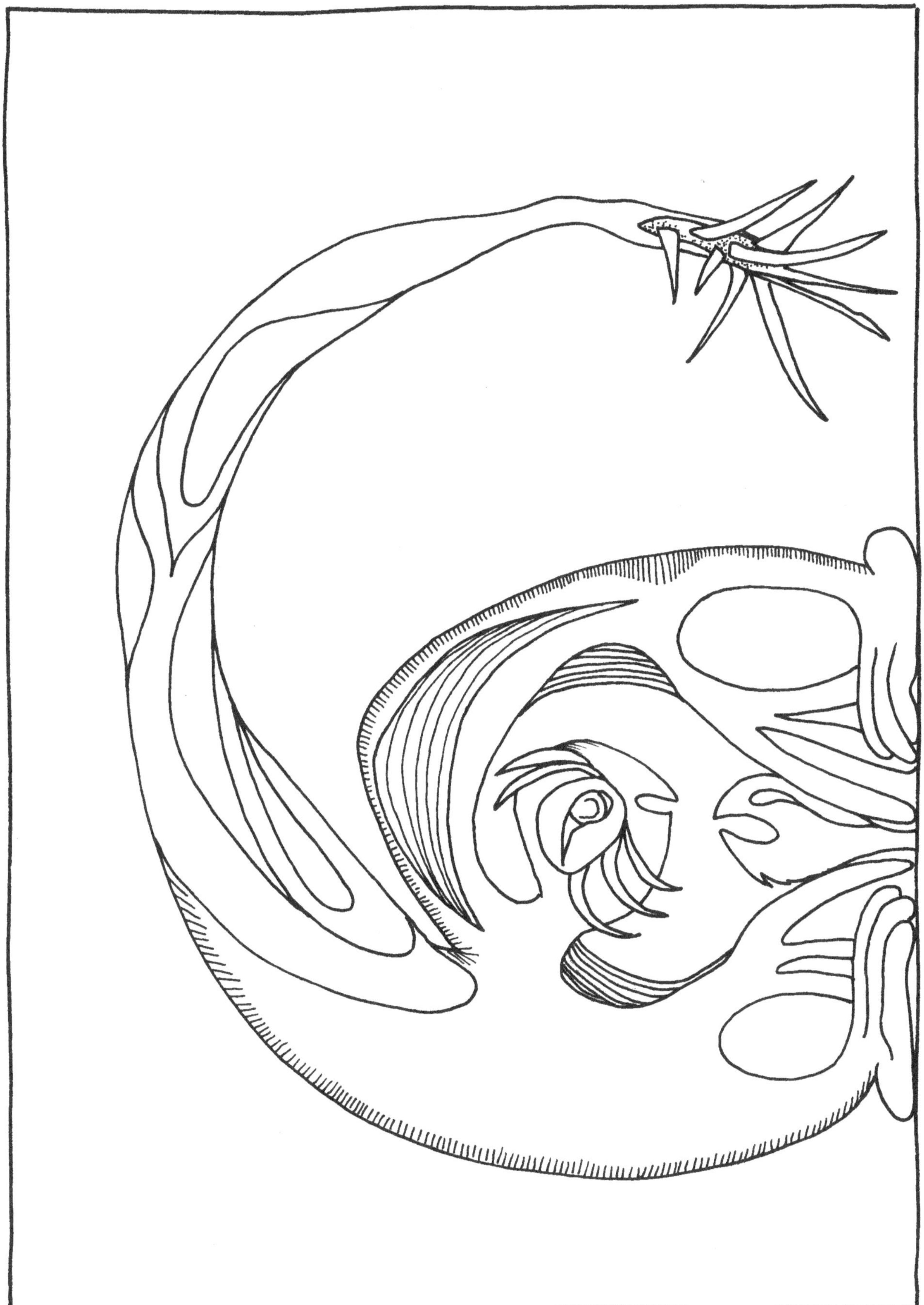

CREATURA #4

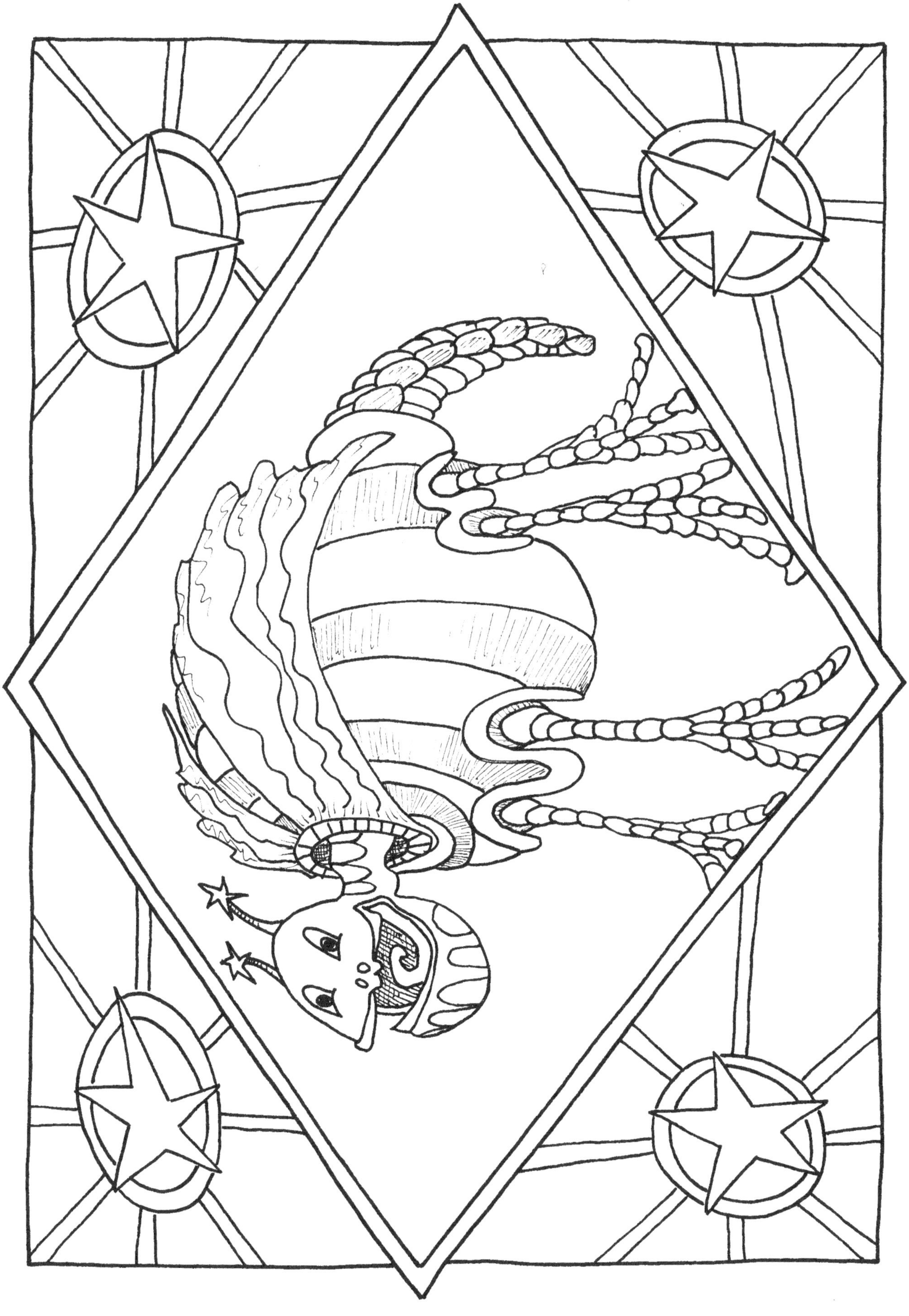

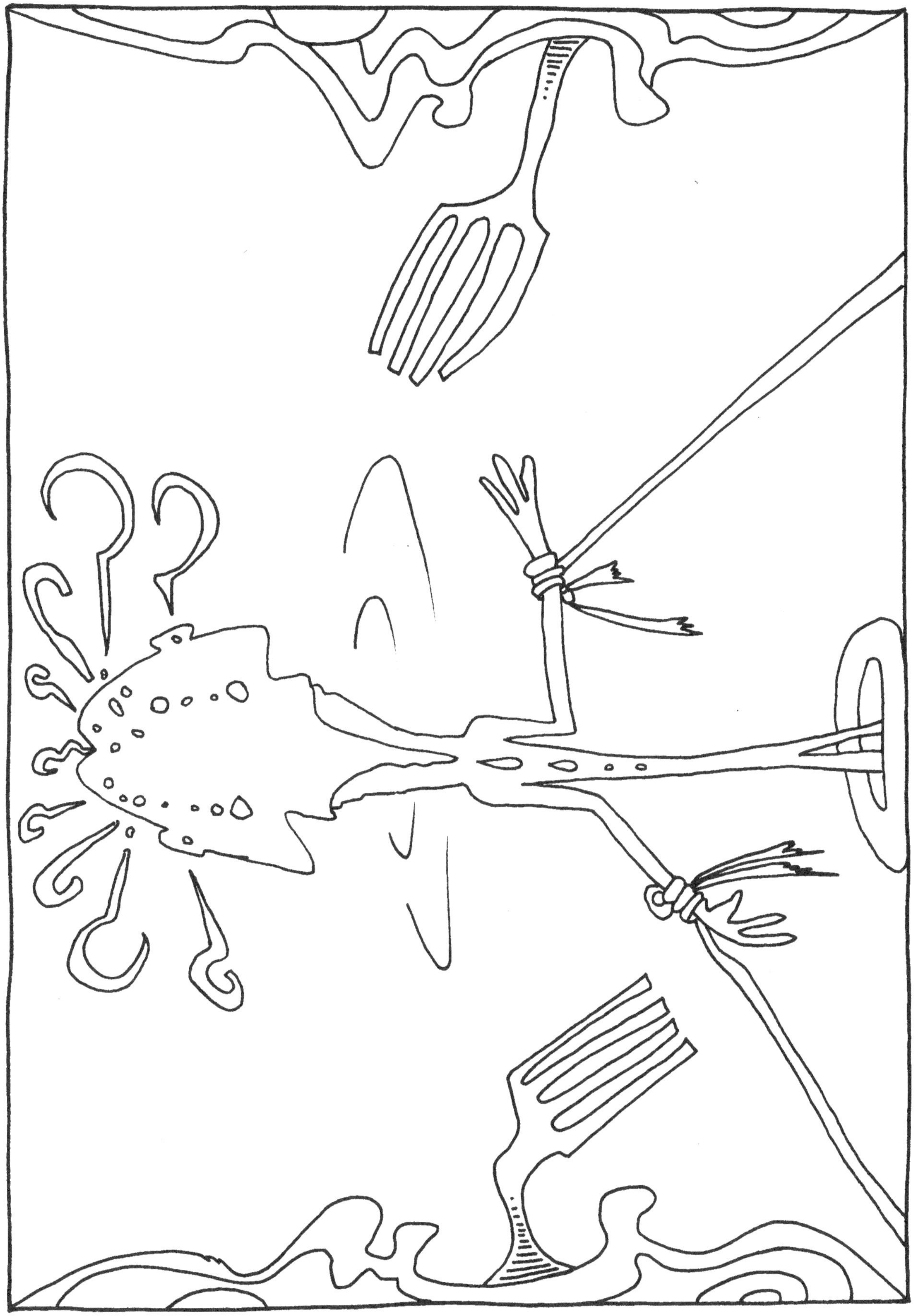

CREATURA #4

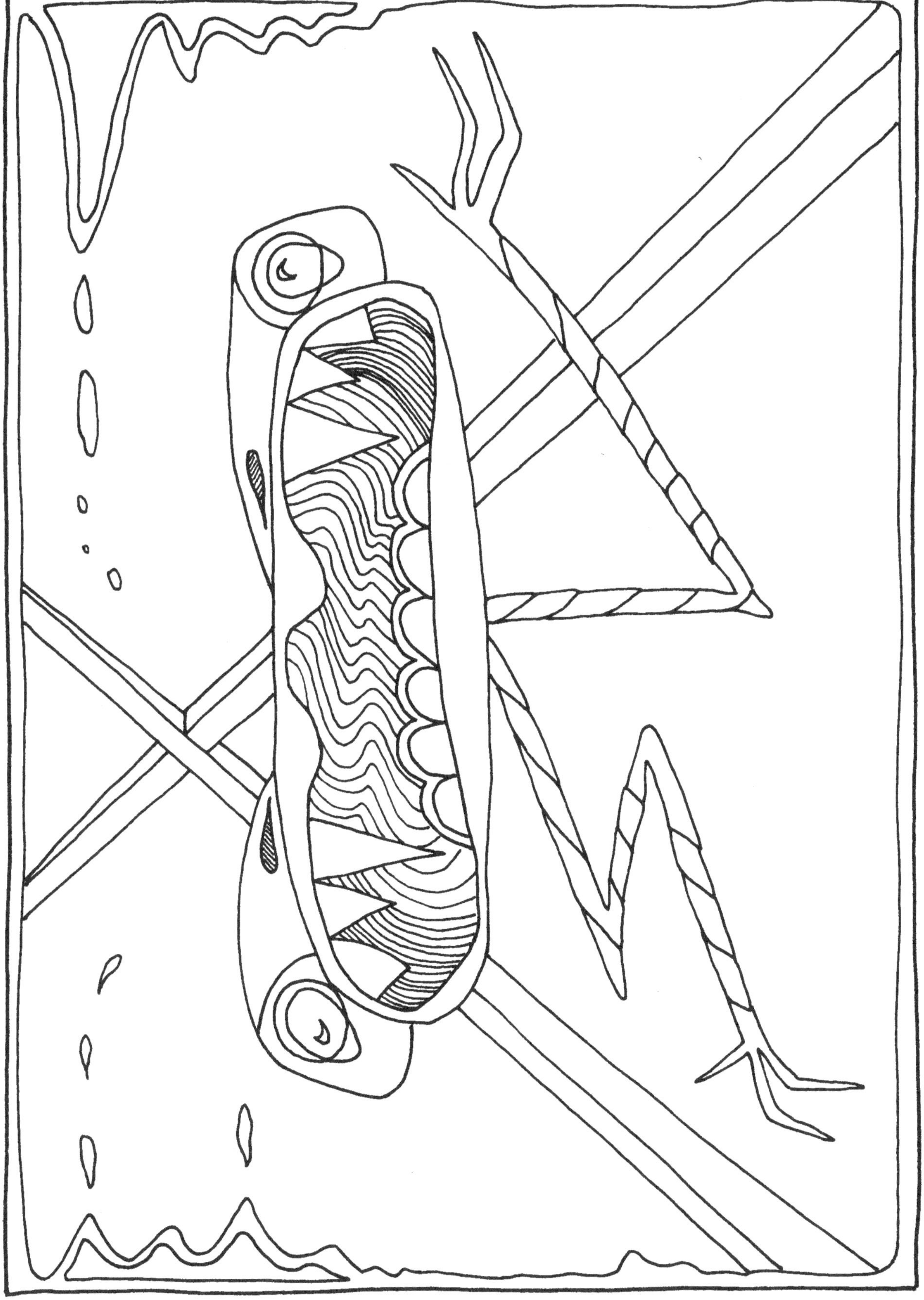

CREATURA #4

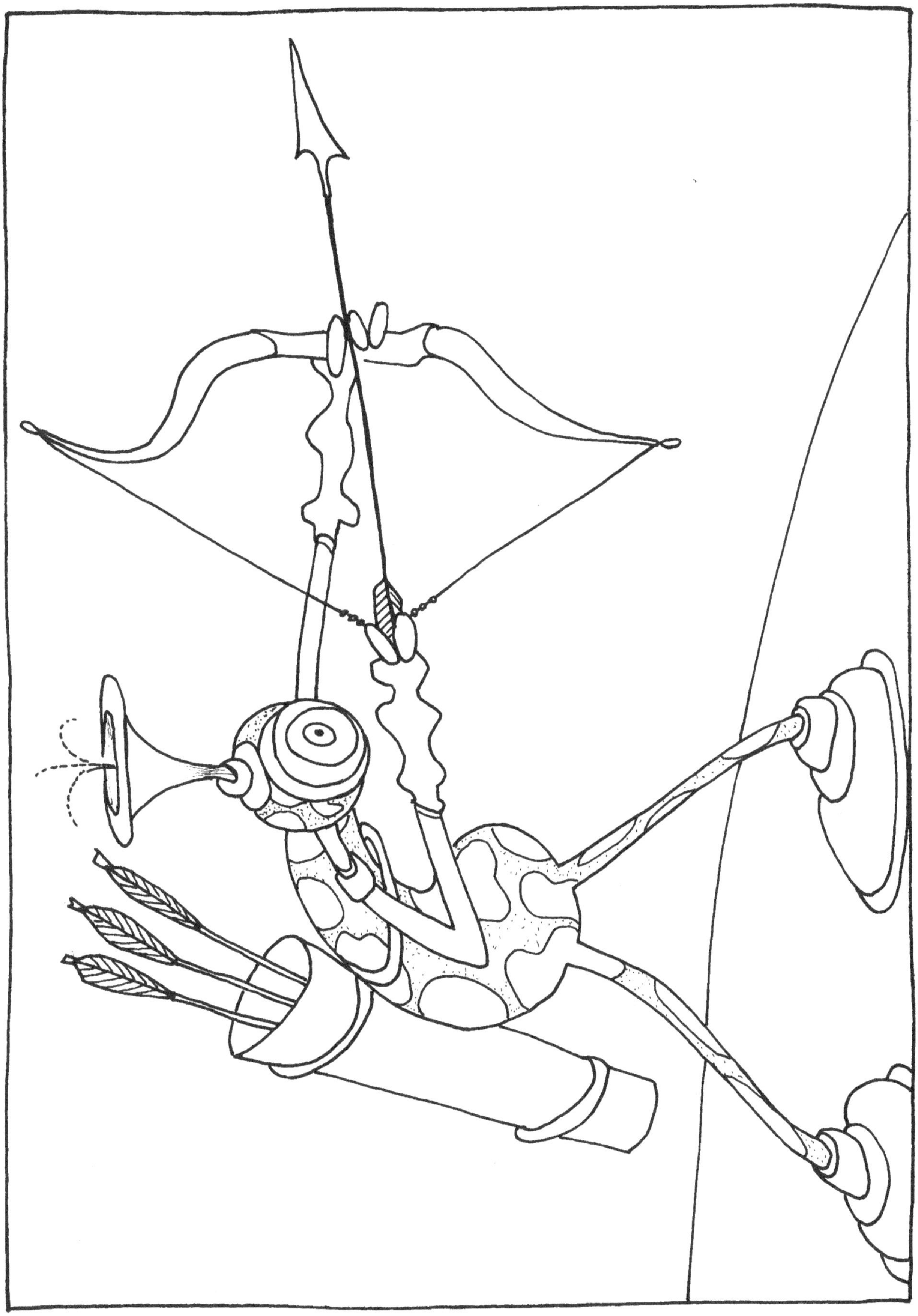

CREATURA #4

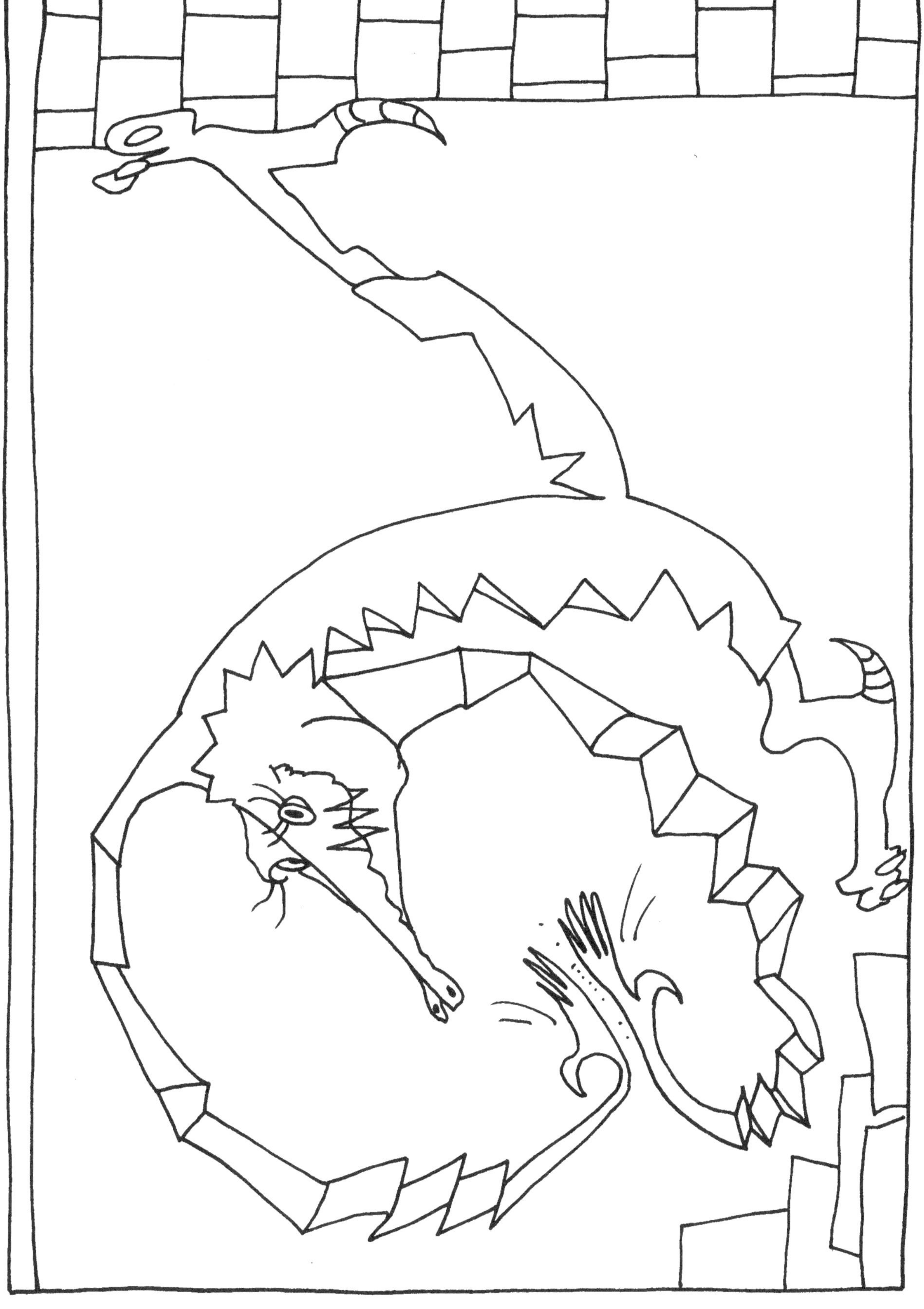

CREATURA #4

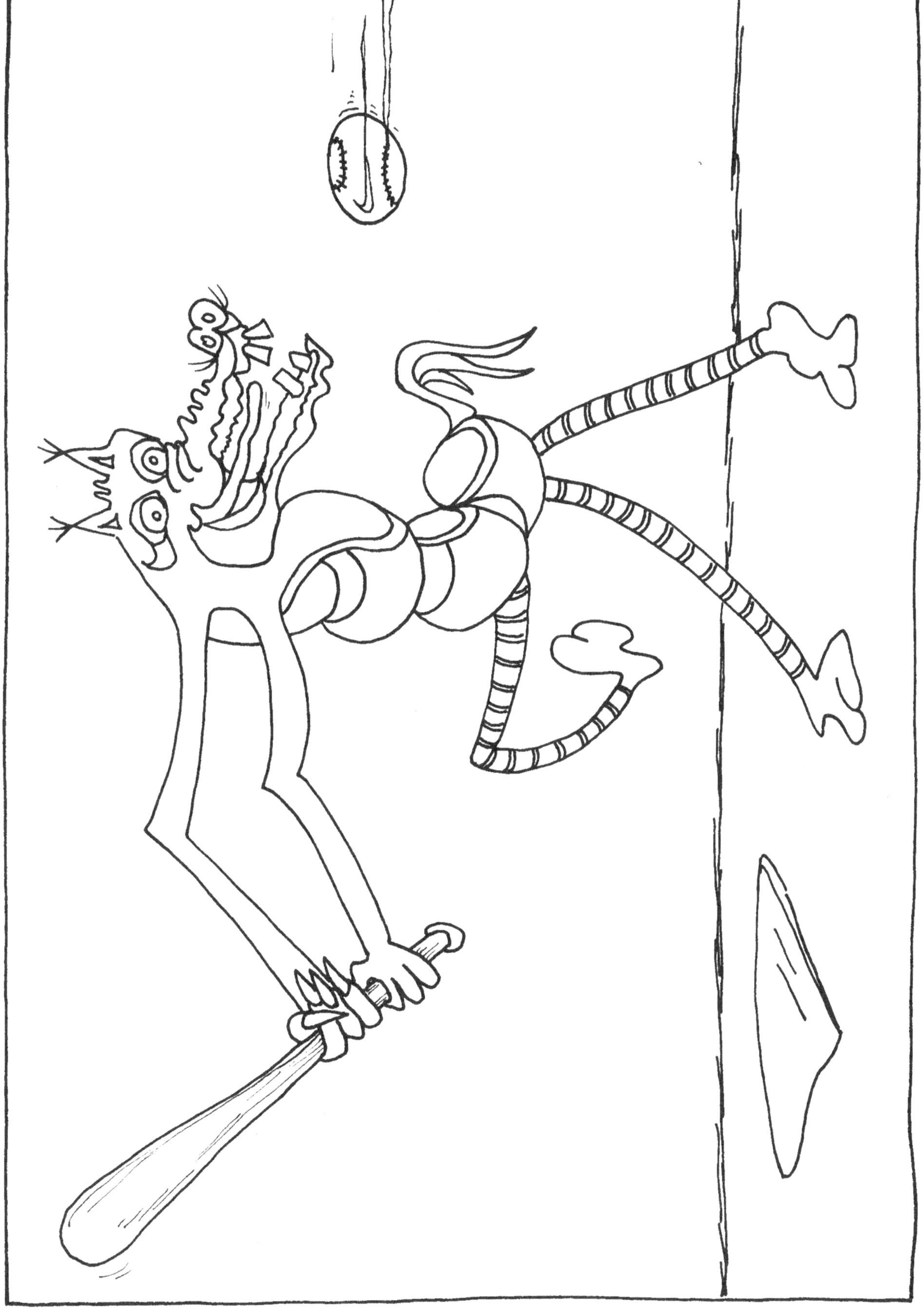

CREATURA #4

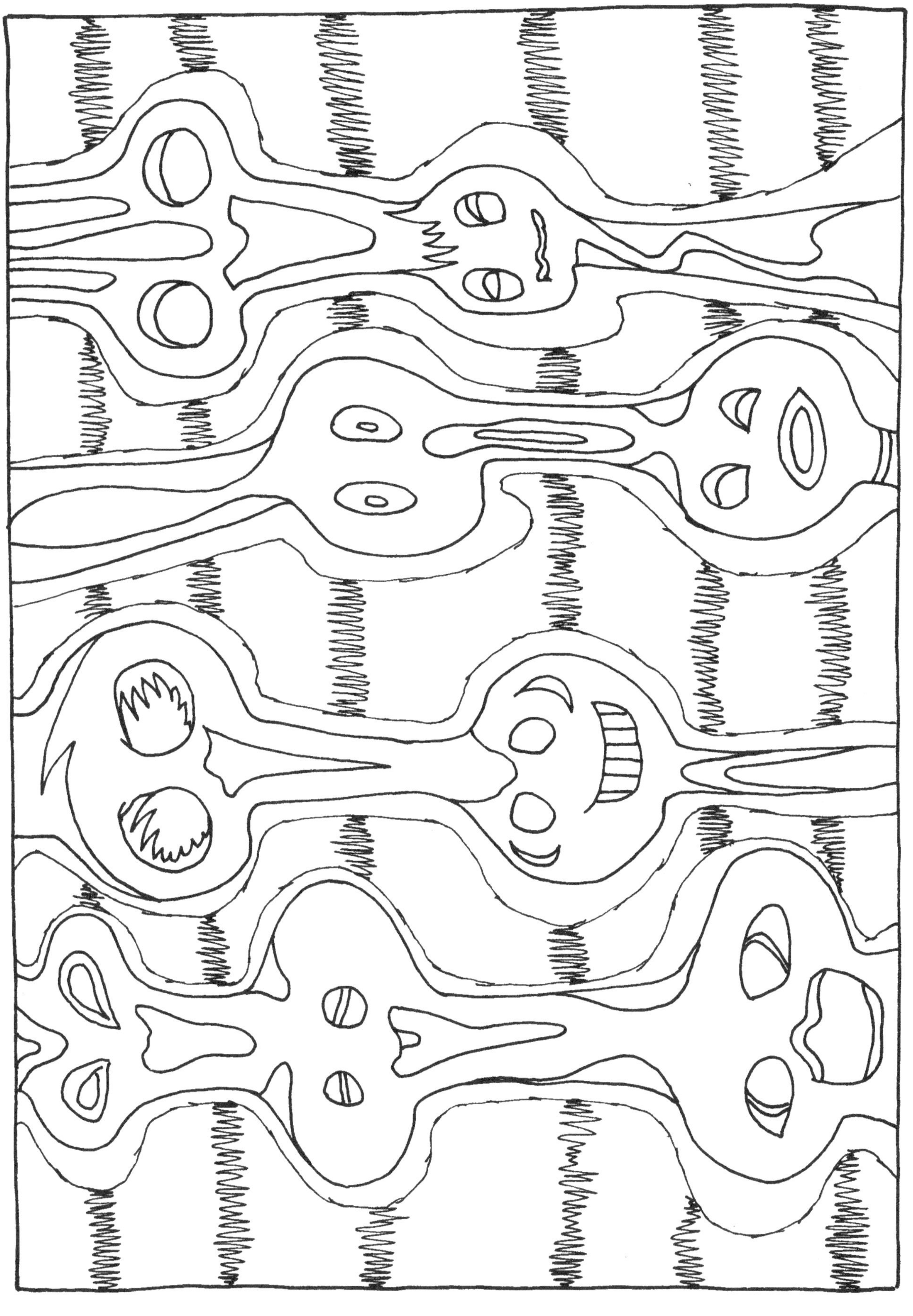

CREATURA #4 ©2018 Joan Worth

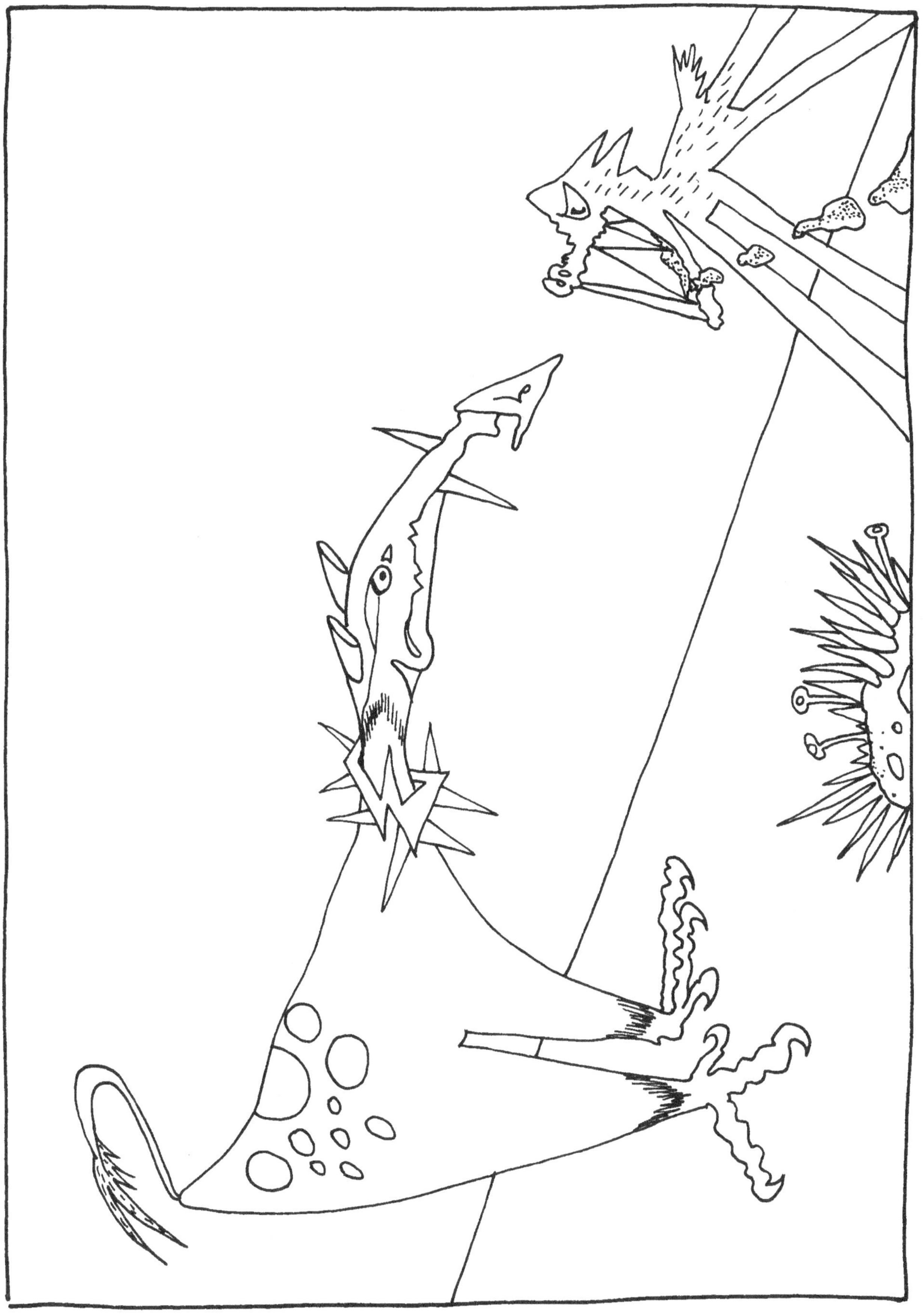

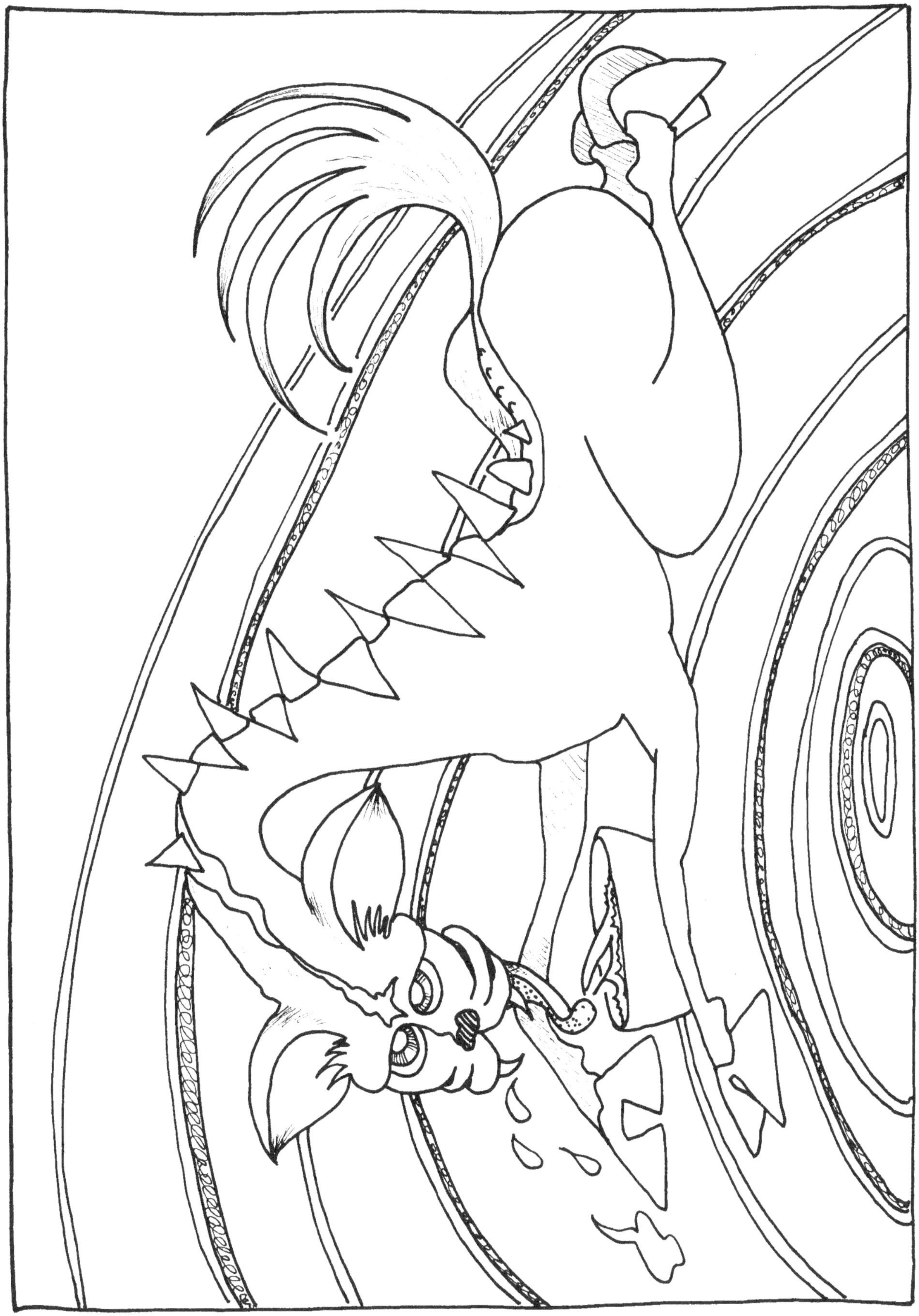

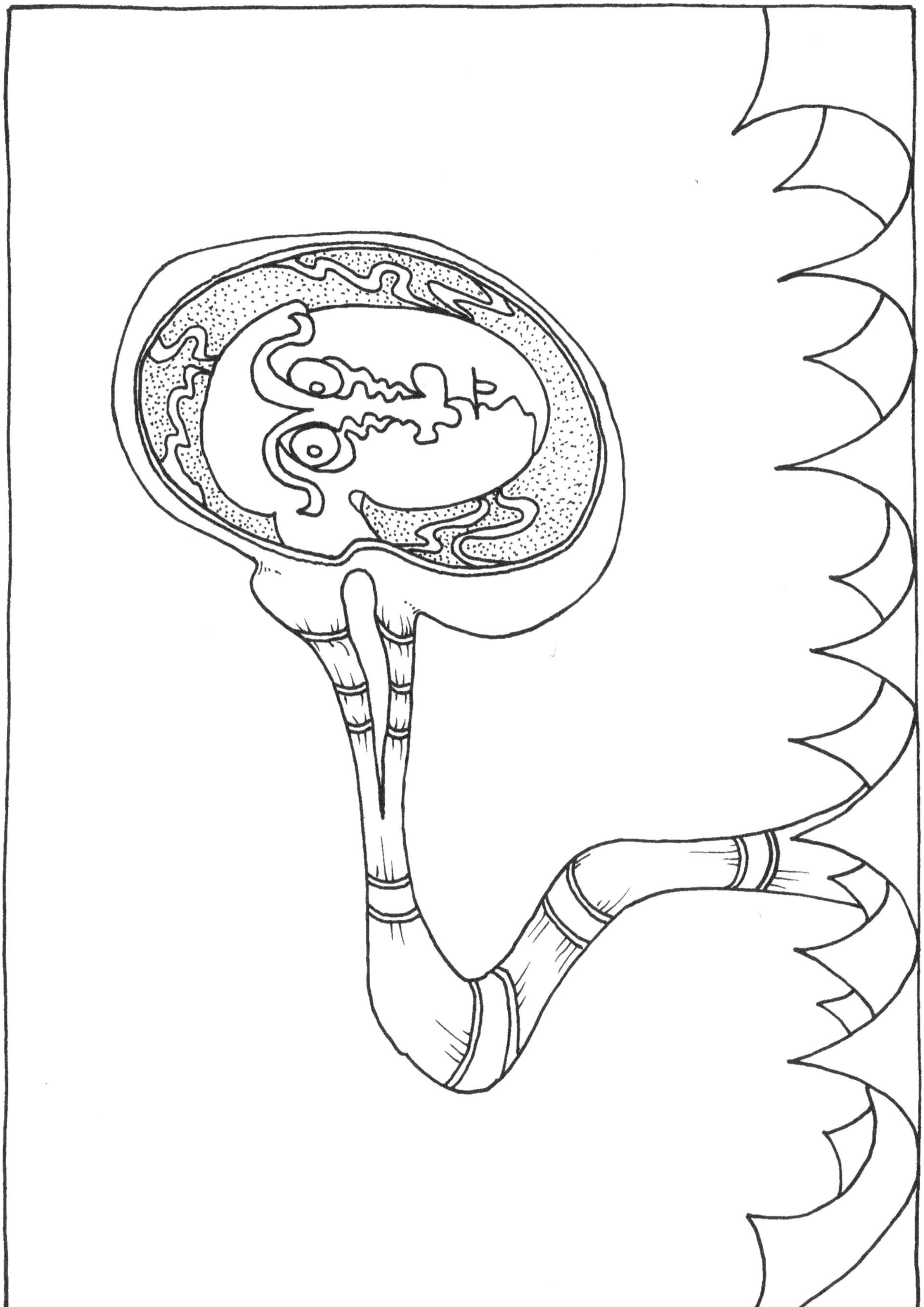

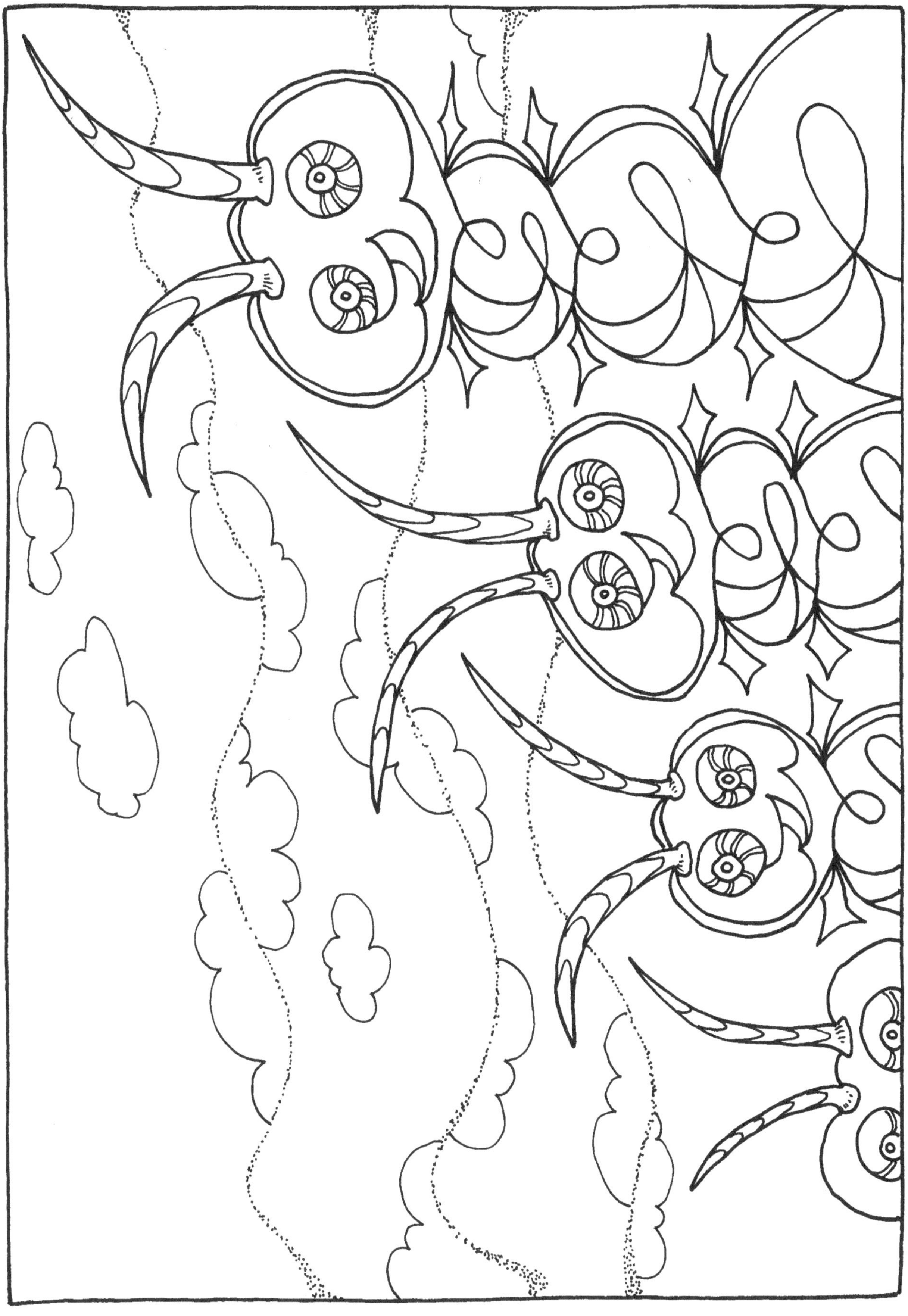

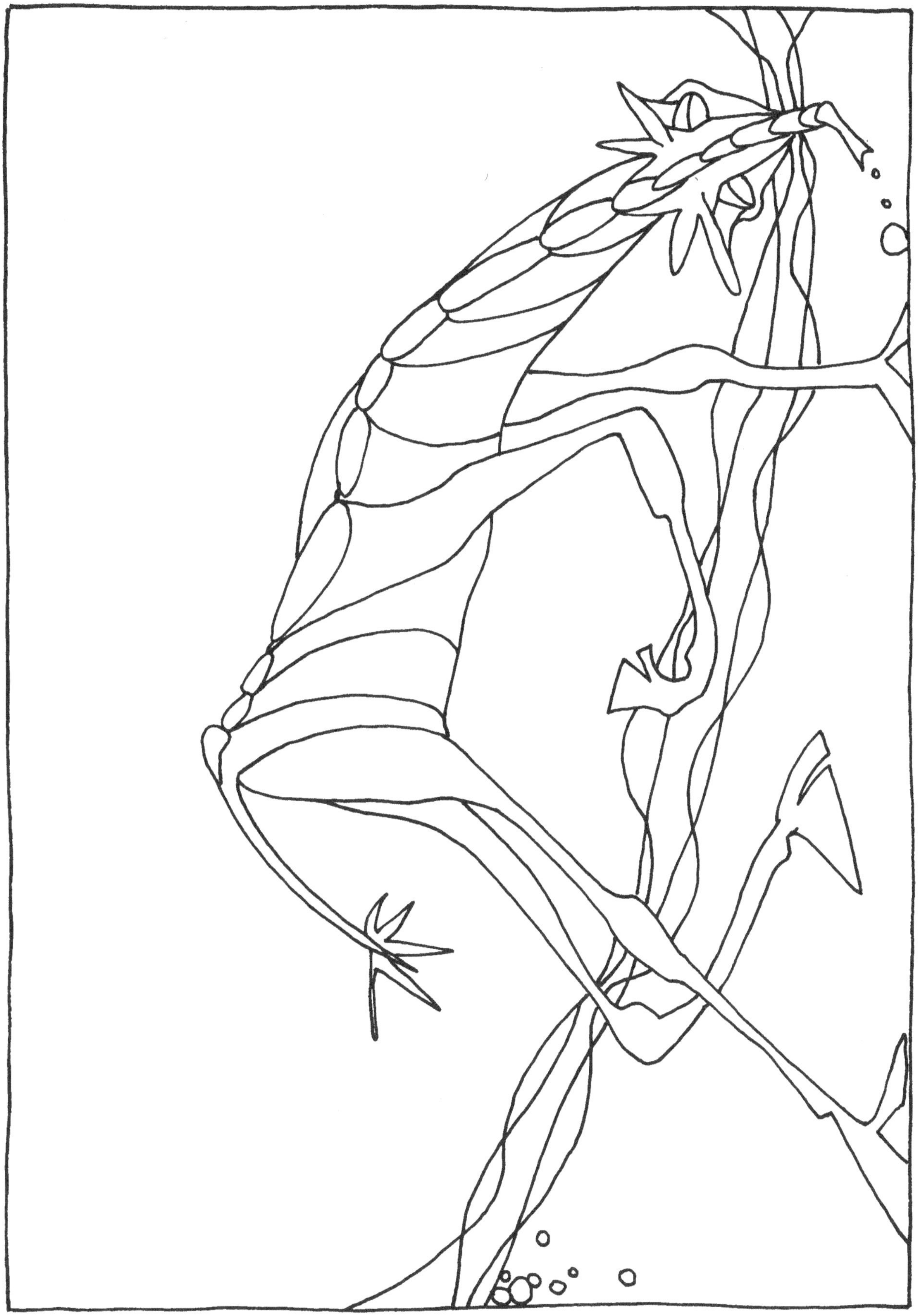

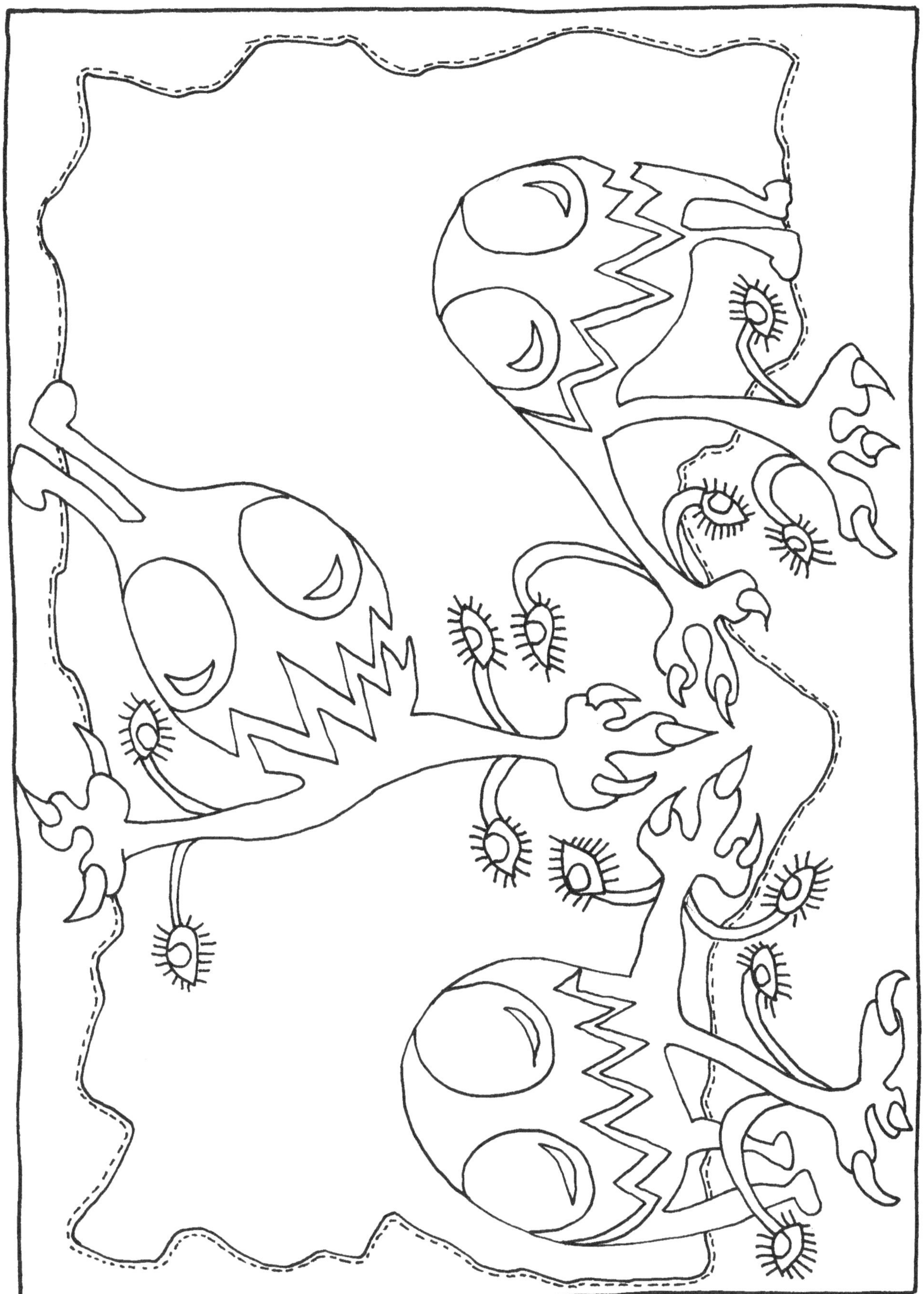

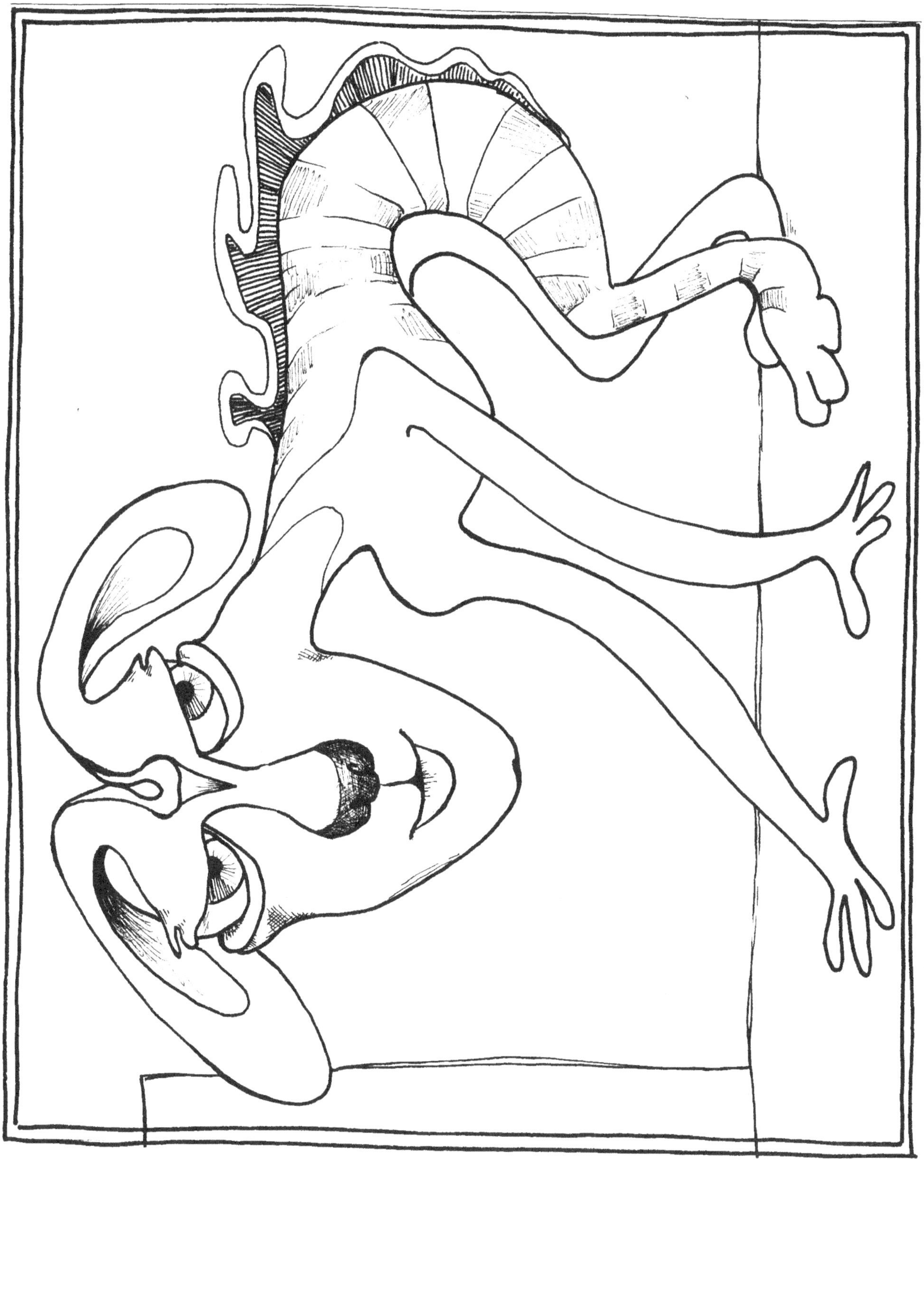

CREATURA #4

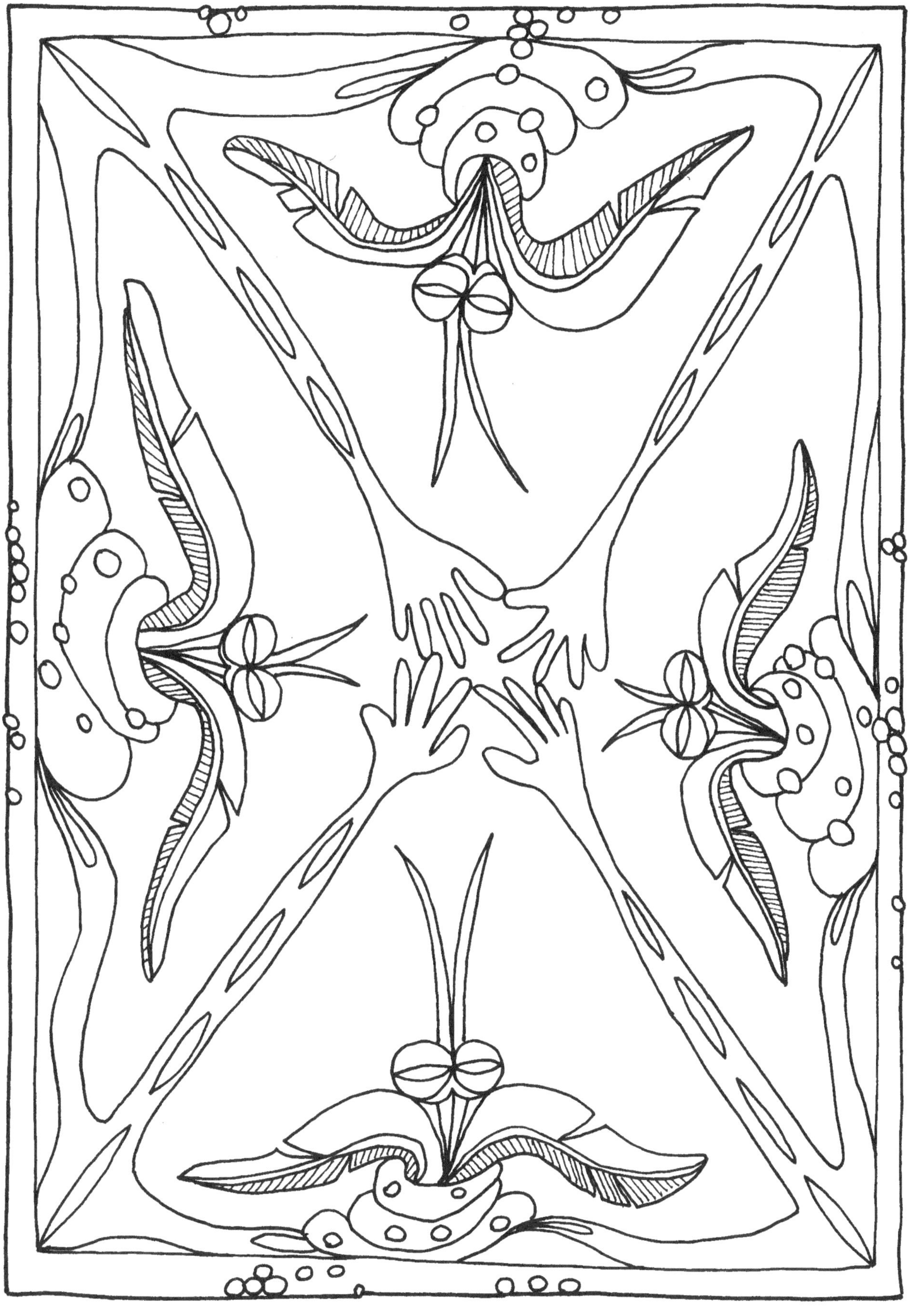

CREATURA #4 ©2018 Joan Worth

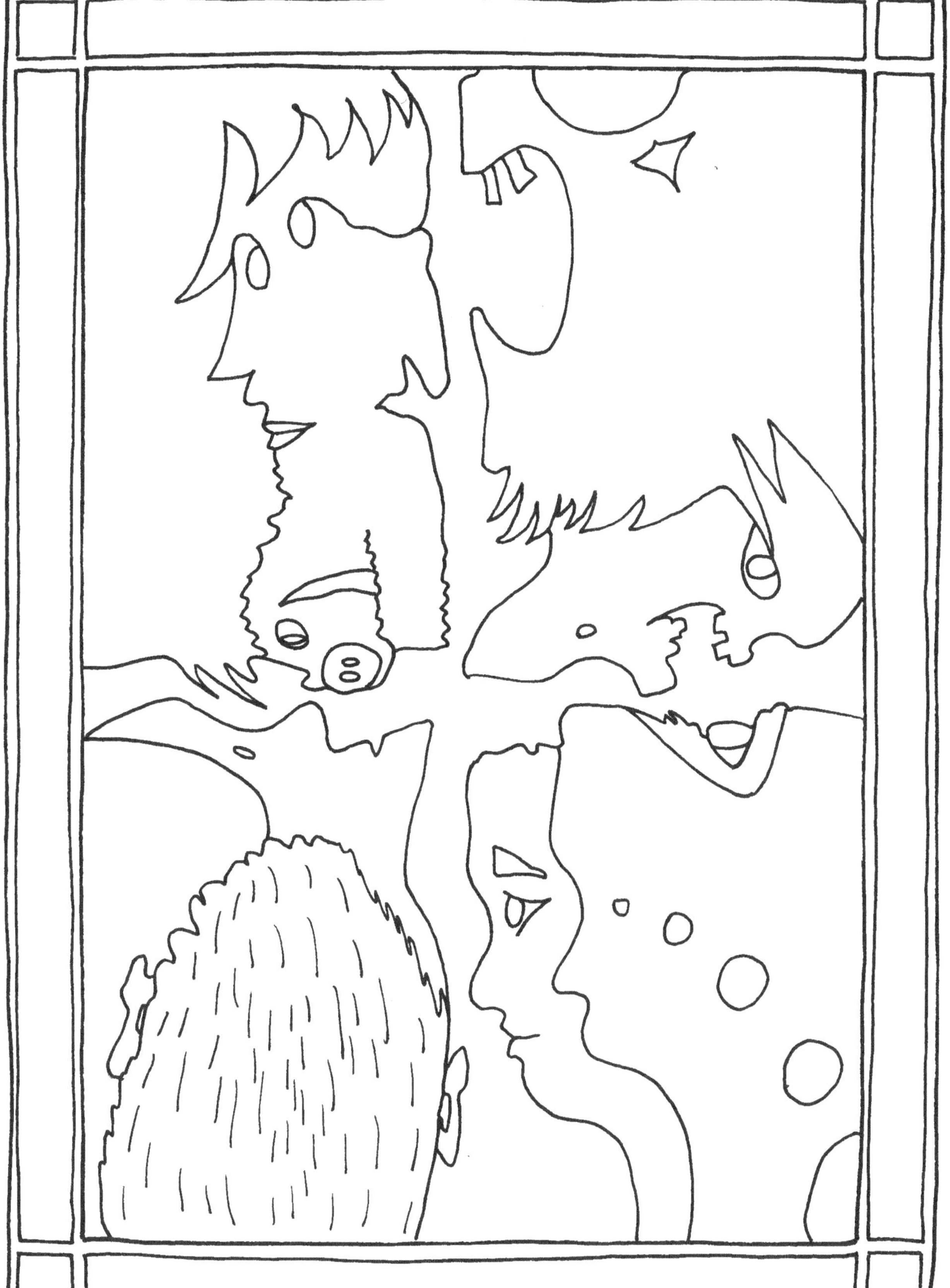

CREATURA #4

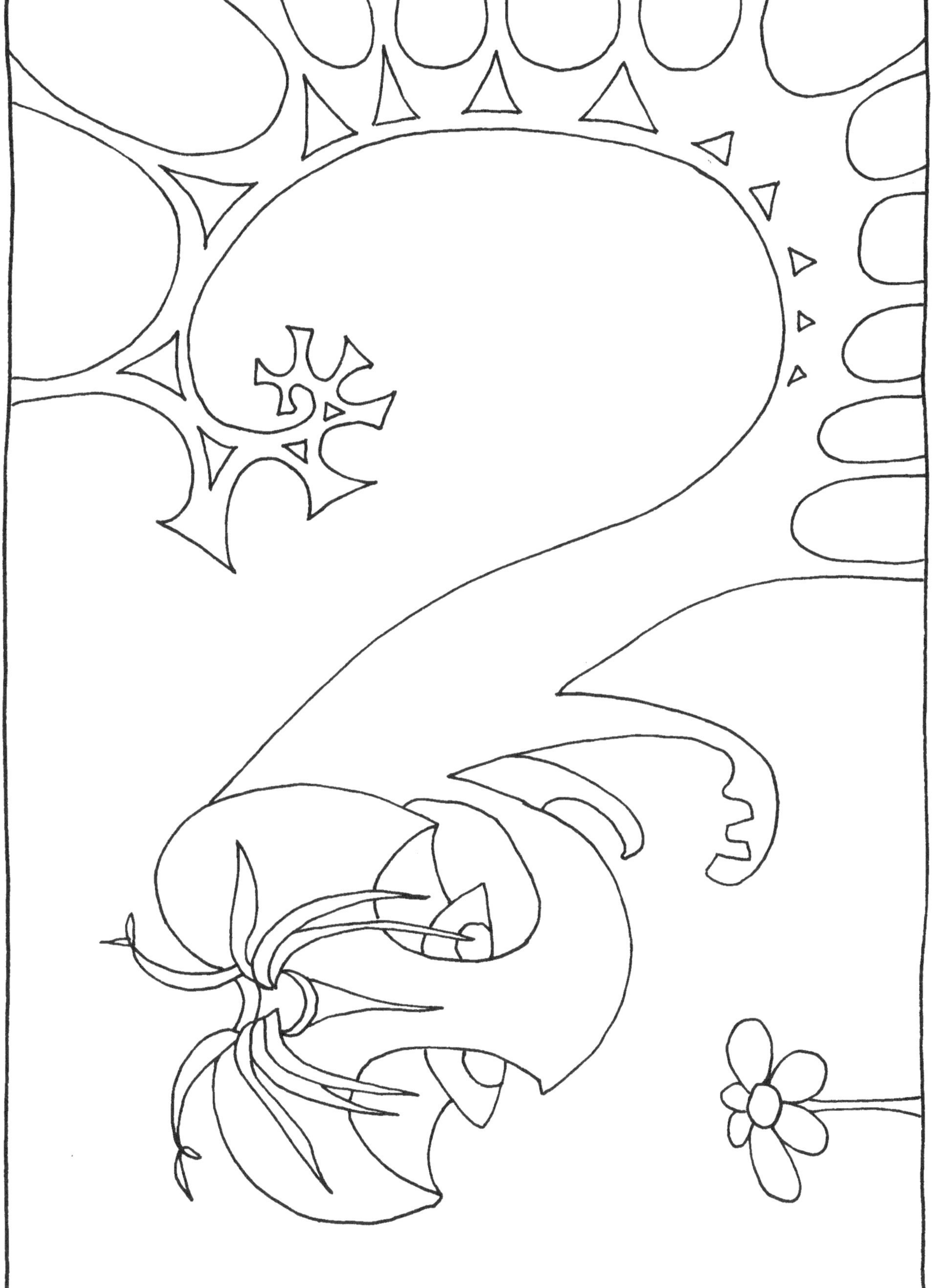

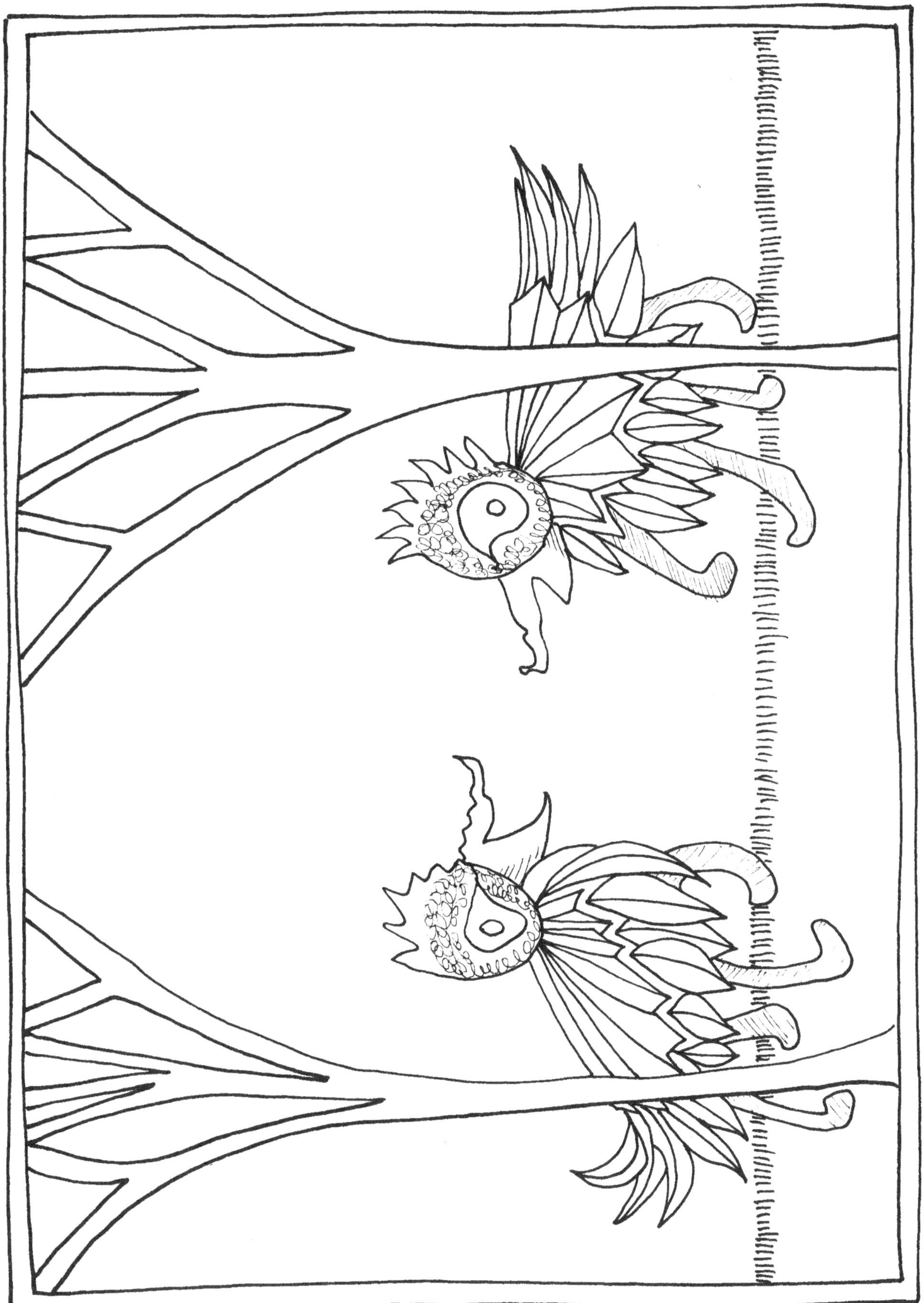

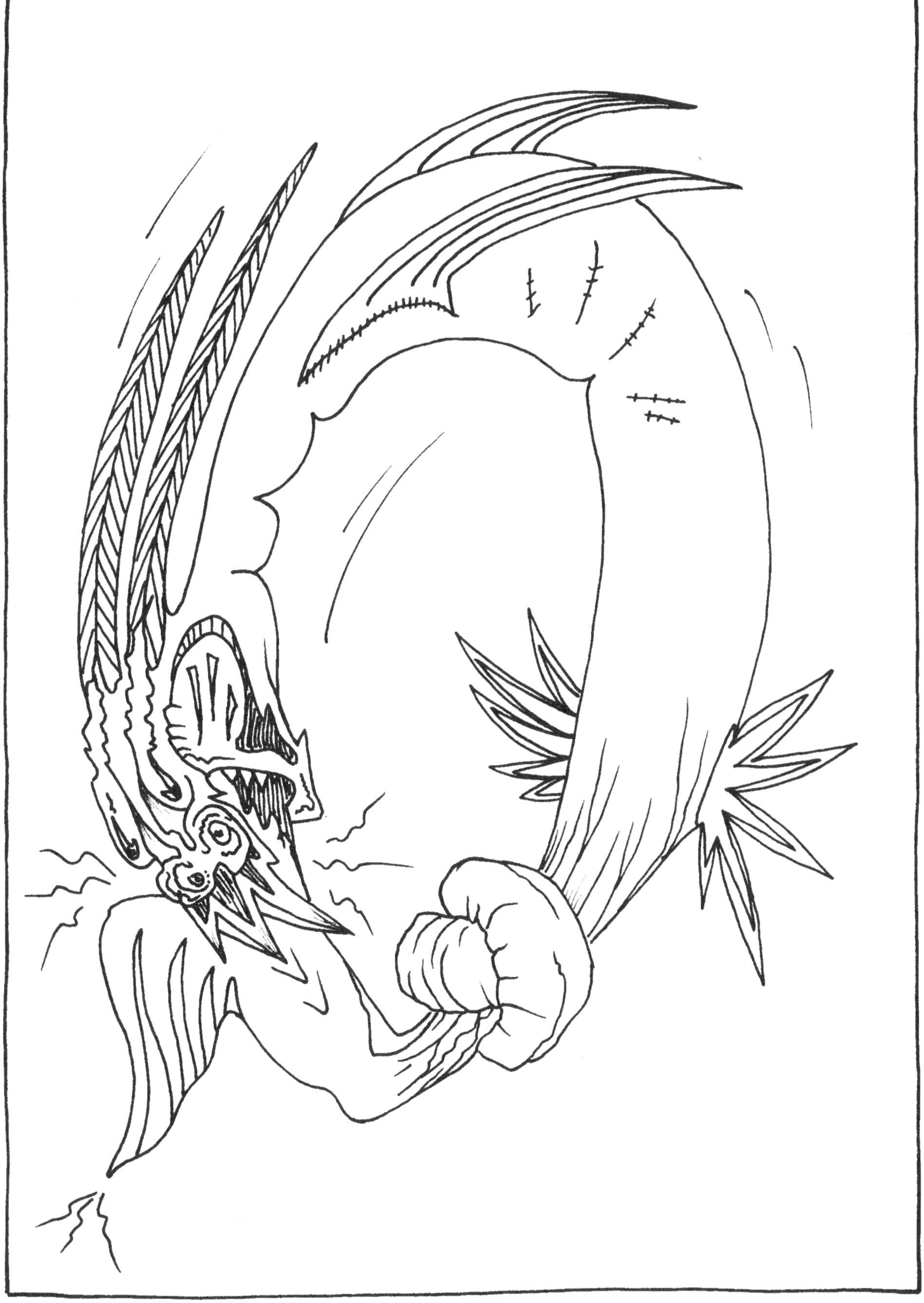

CREATURA #4

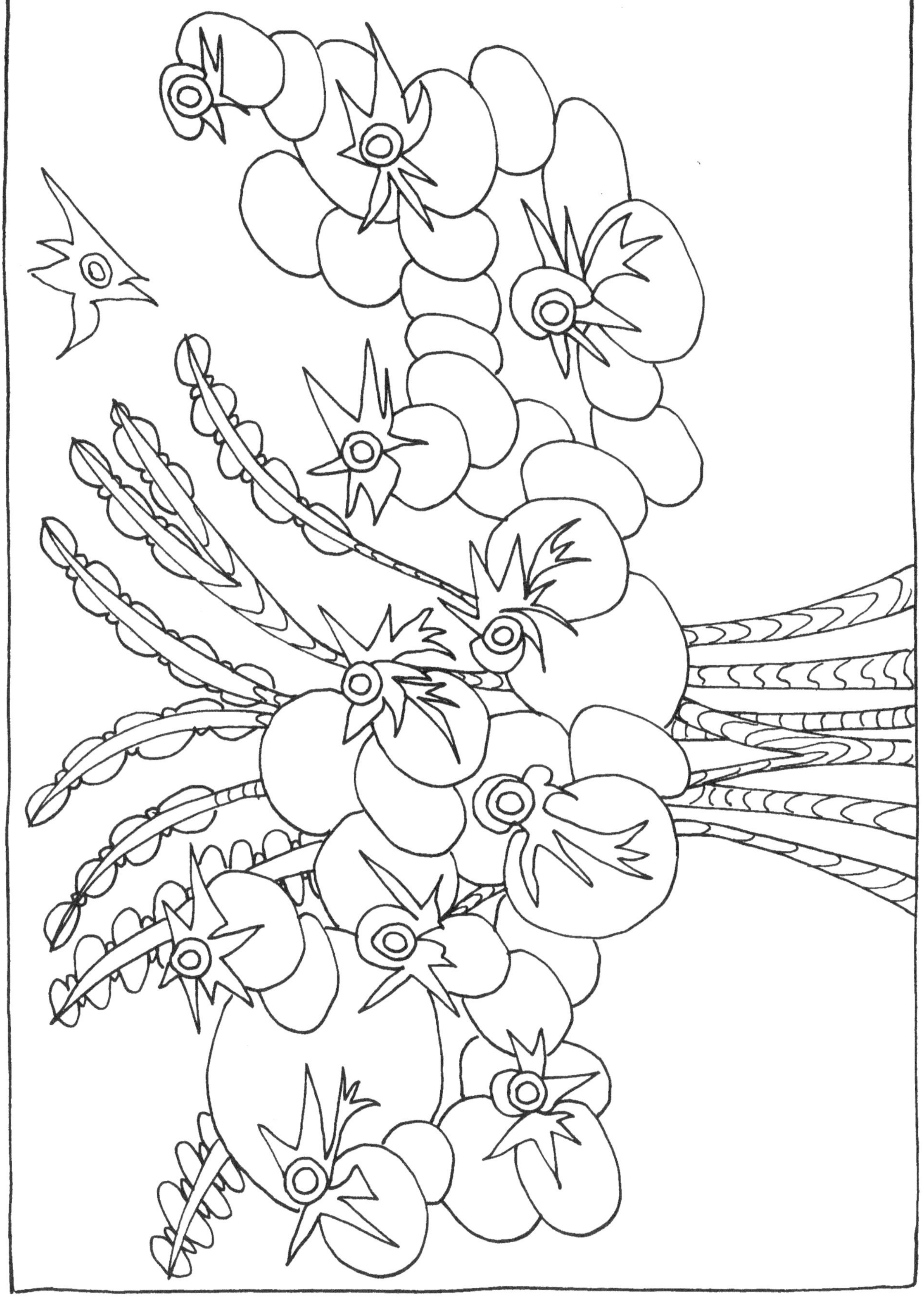

CREATURA #4

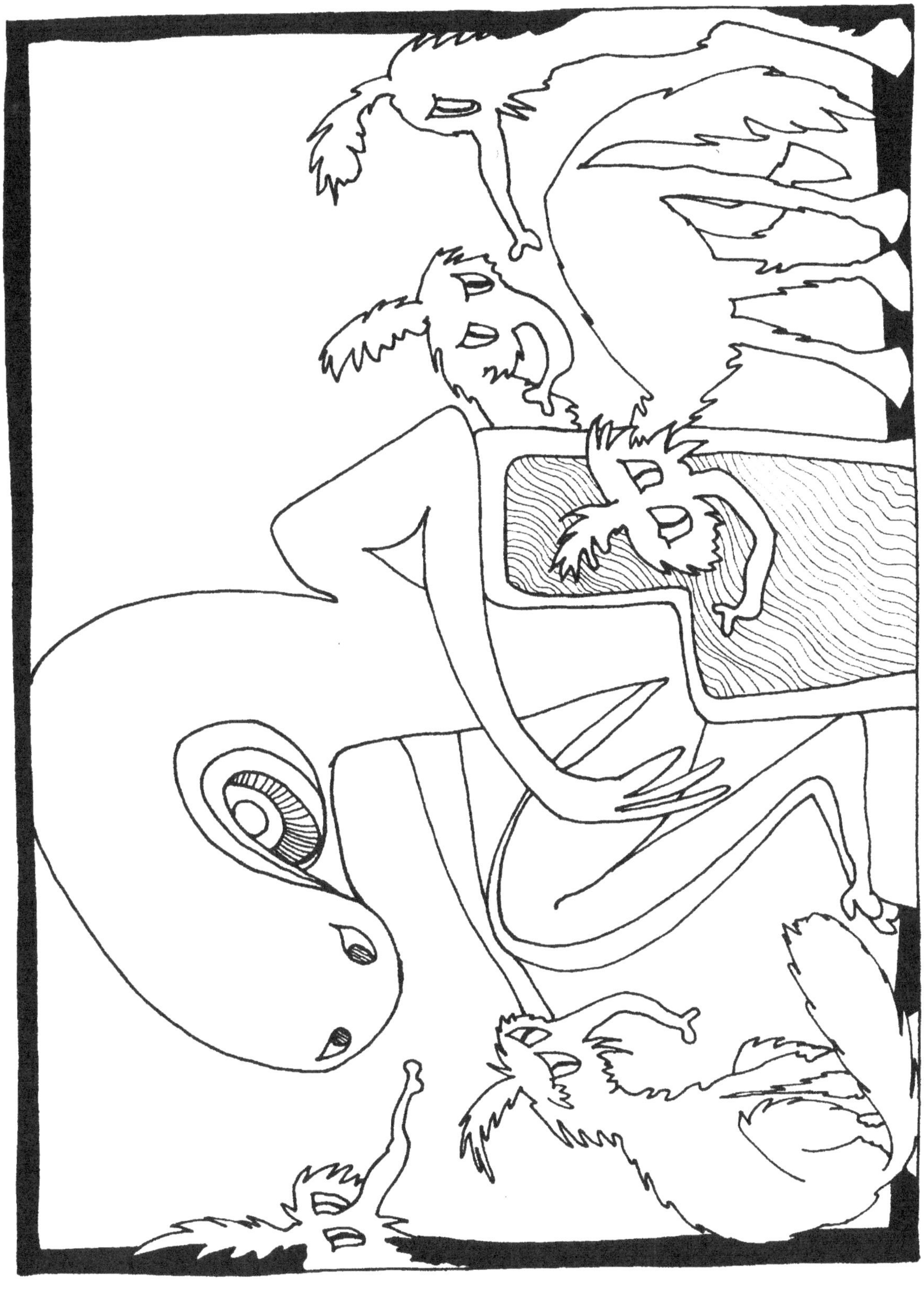

CREATURA #4

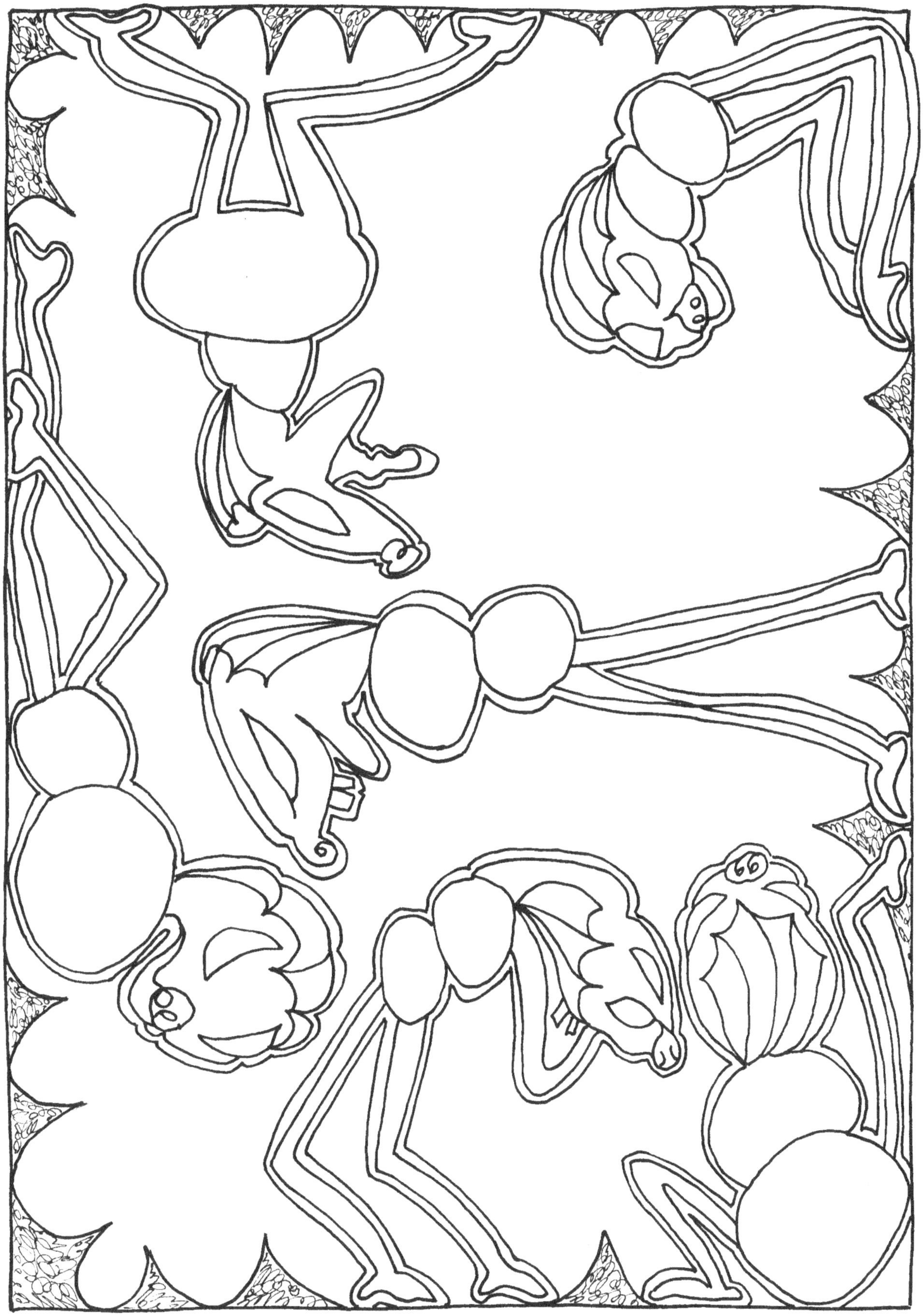

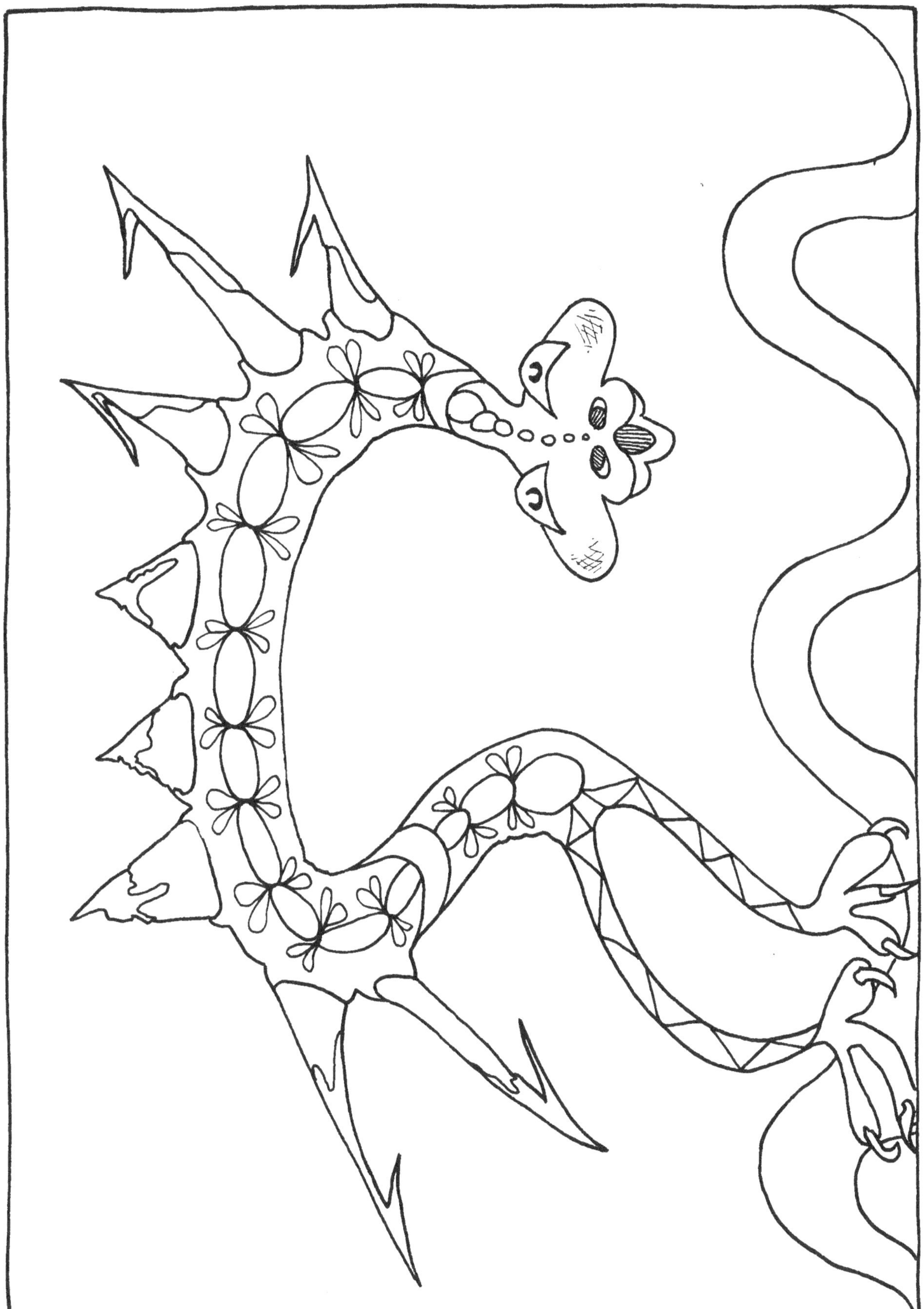

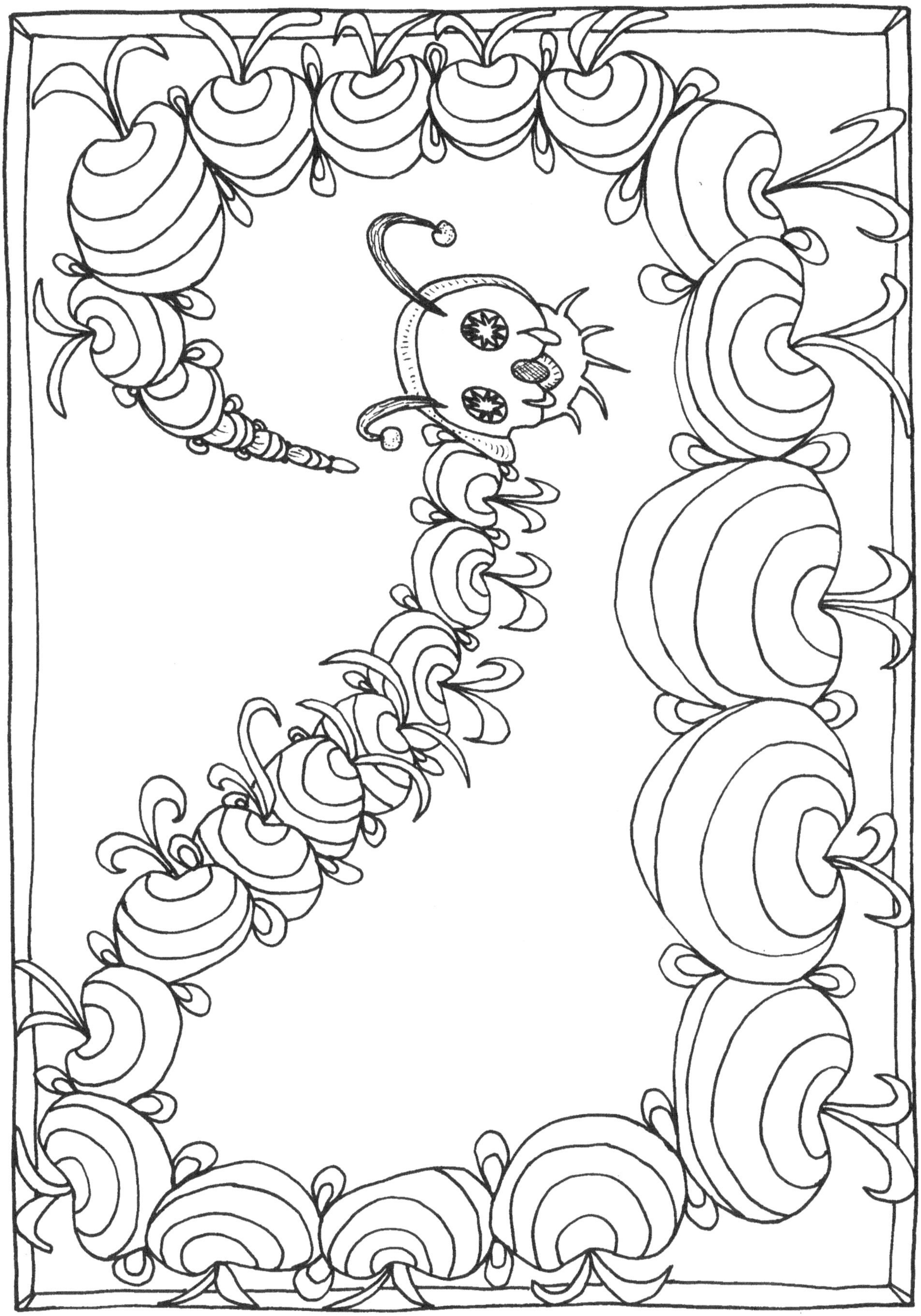

CREATURA #4

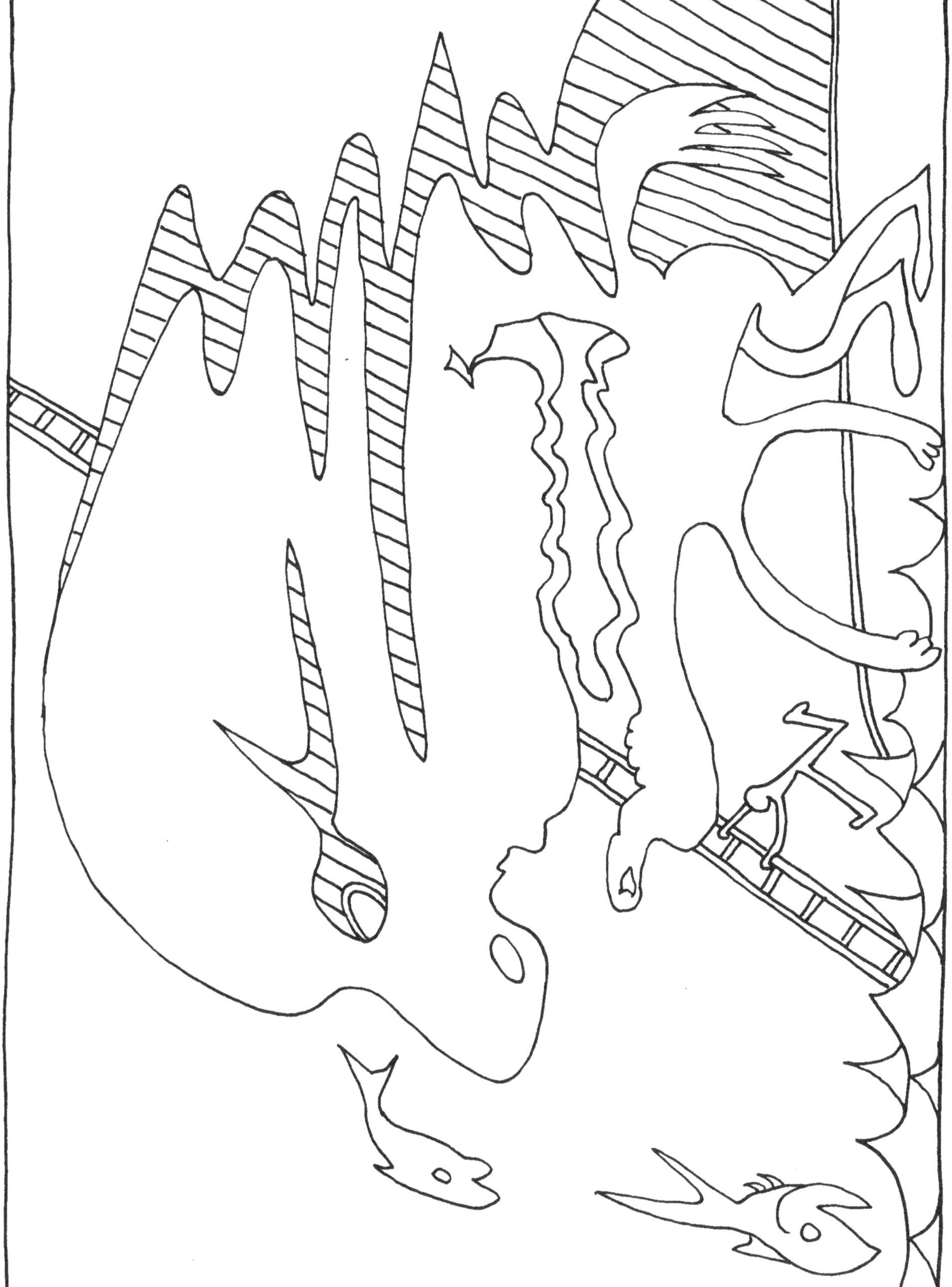

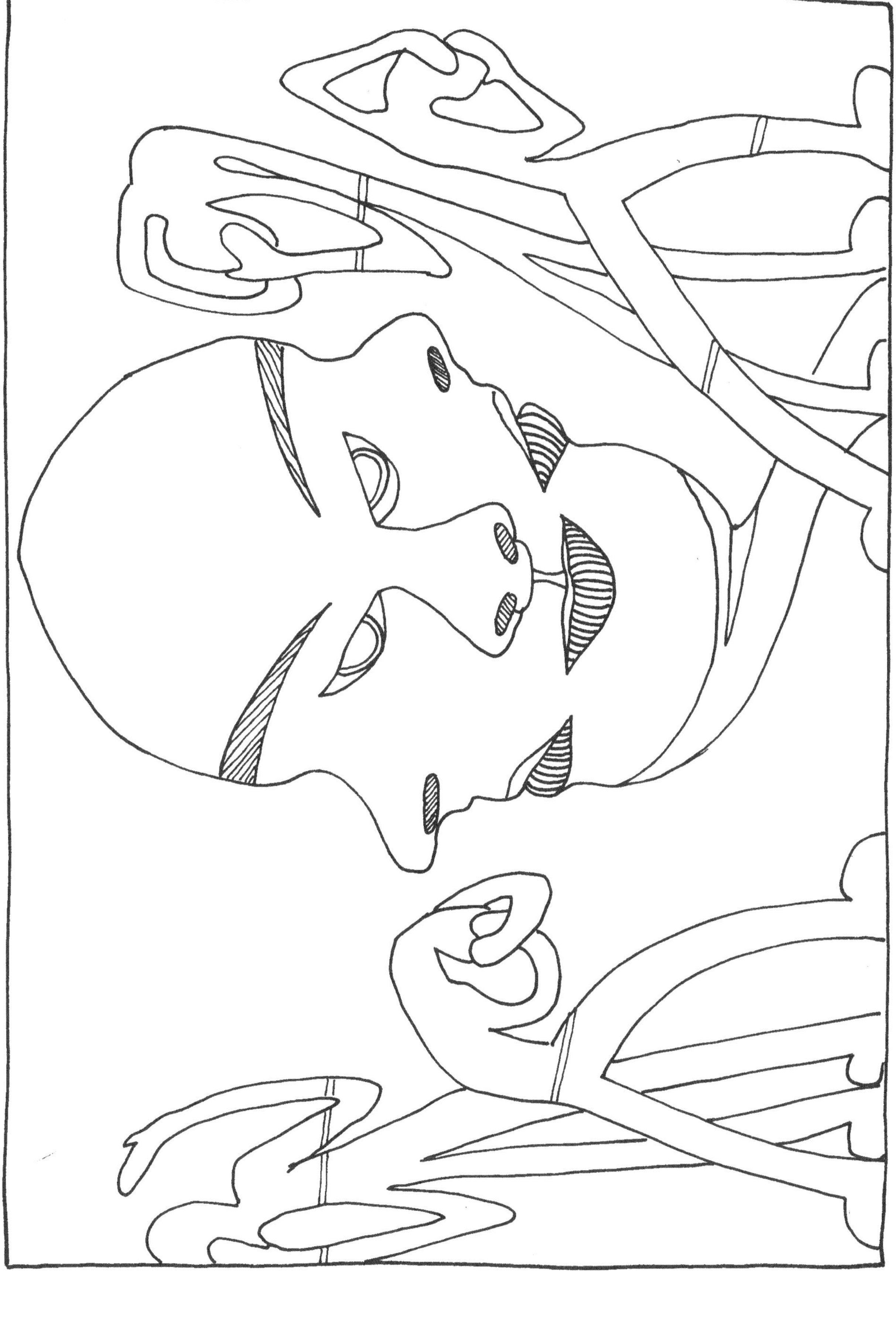

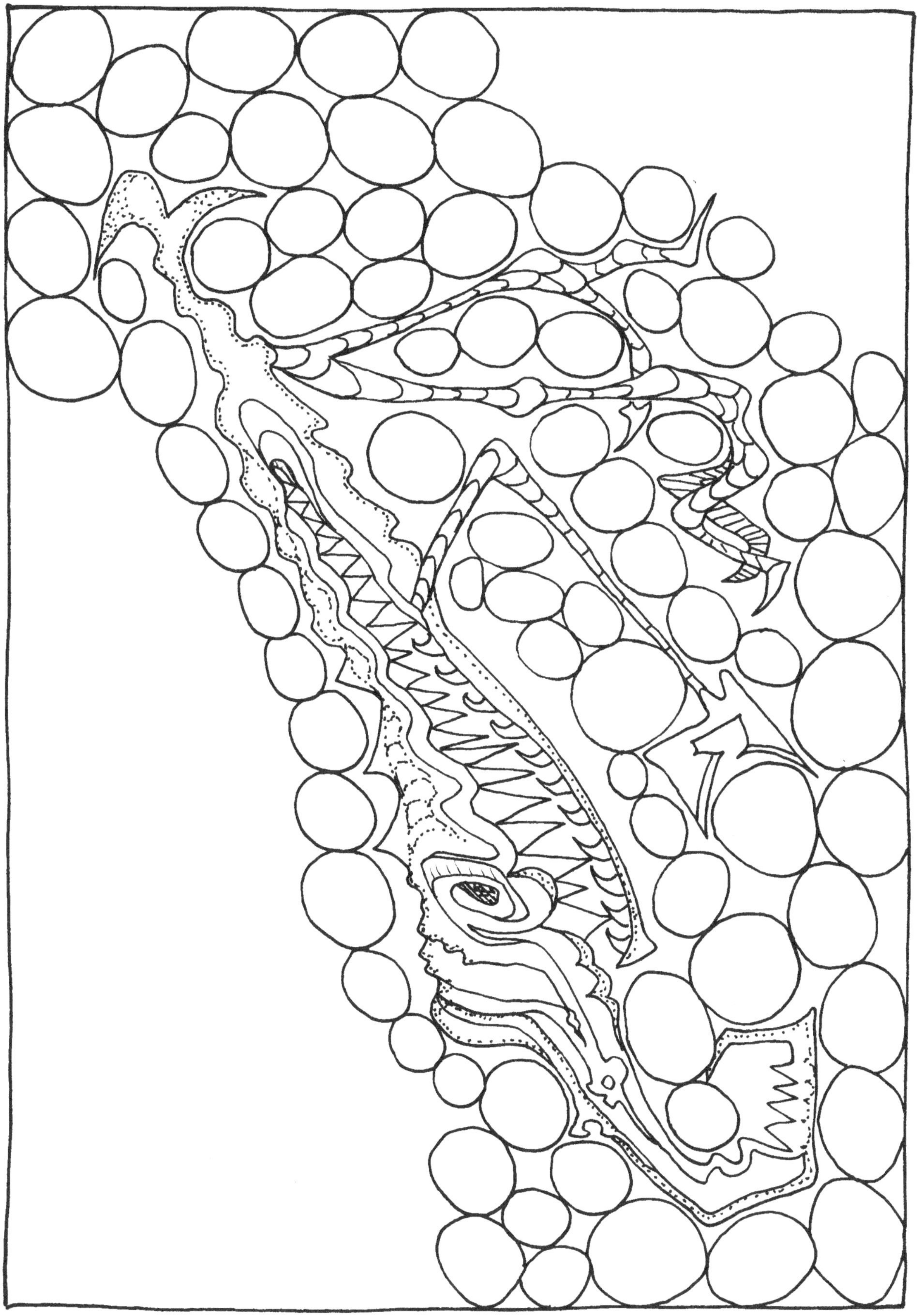

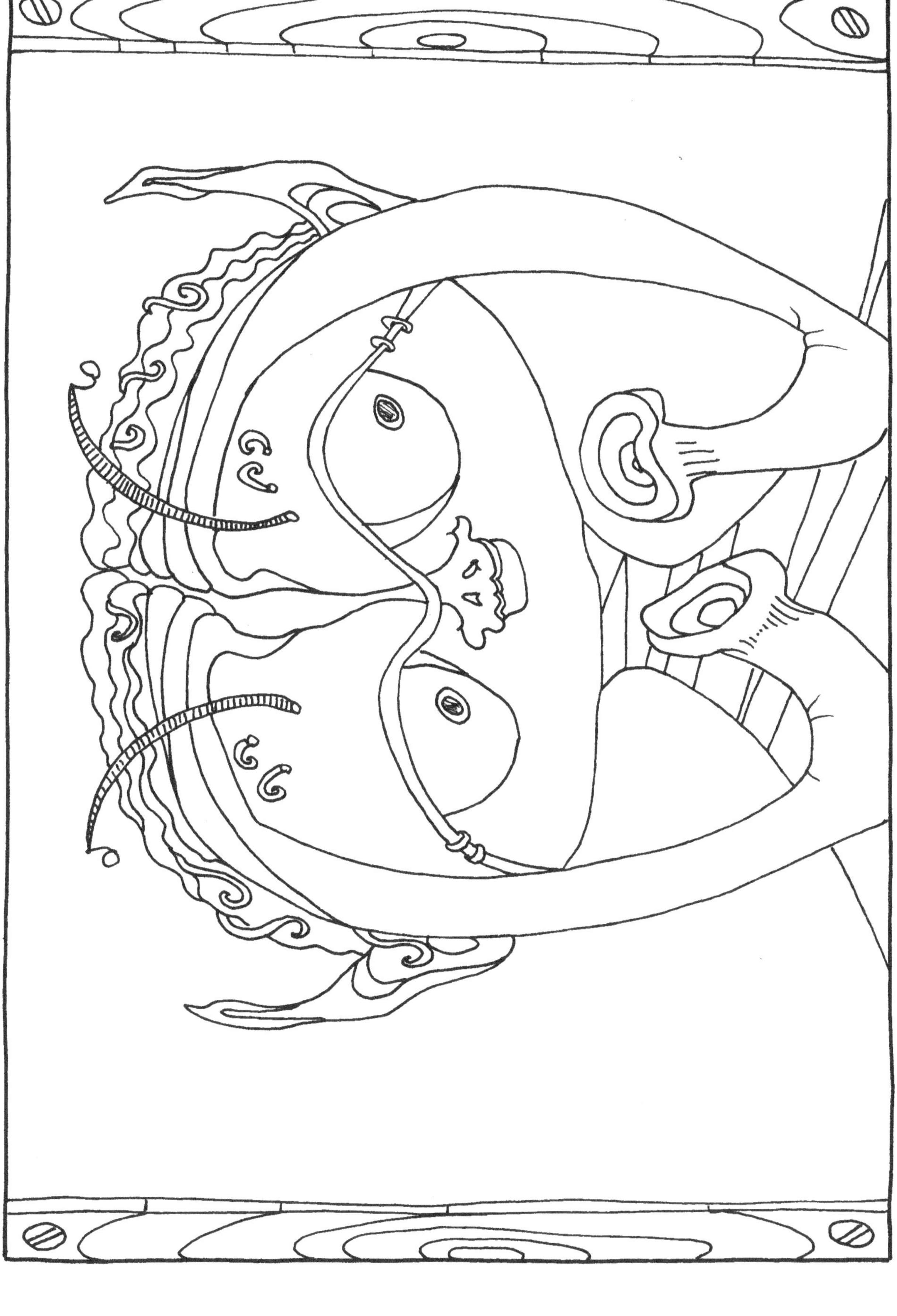

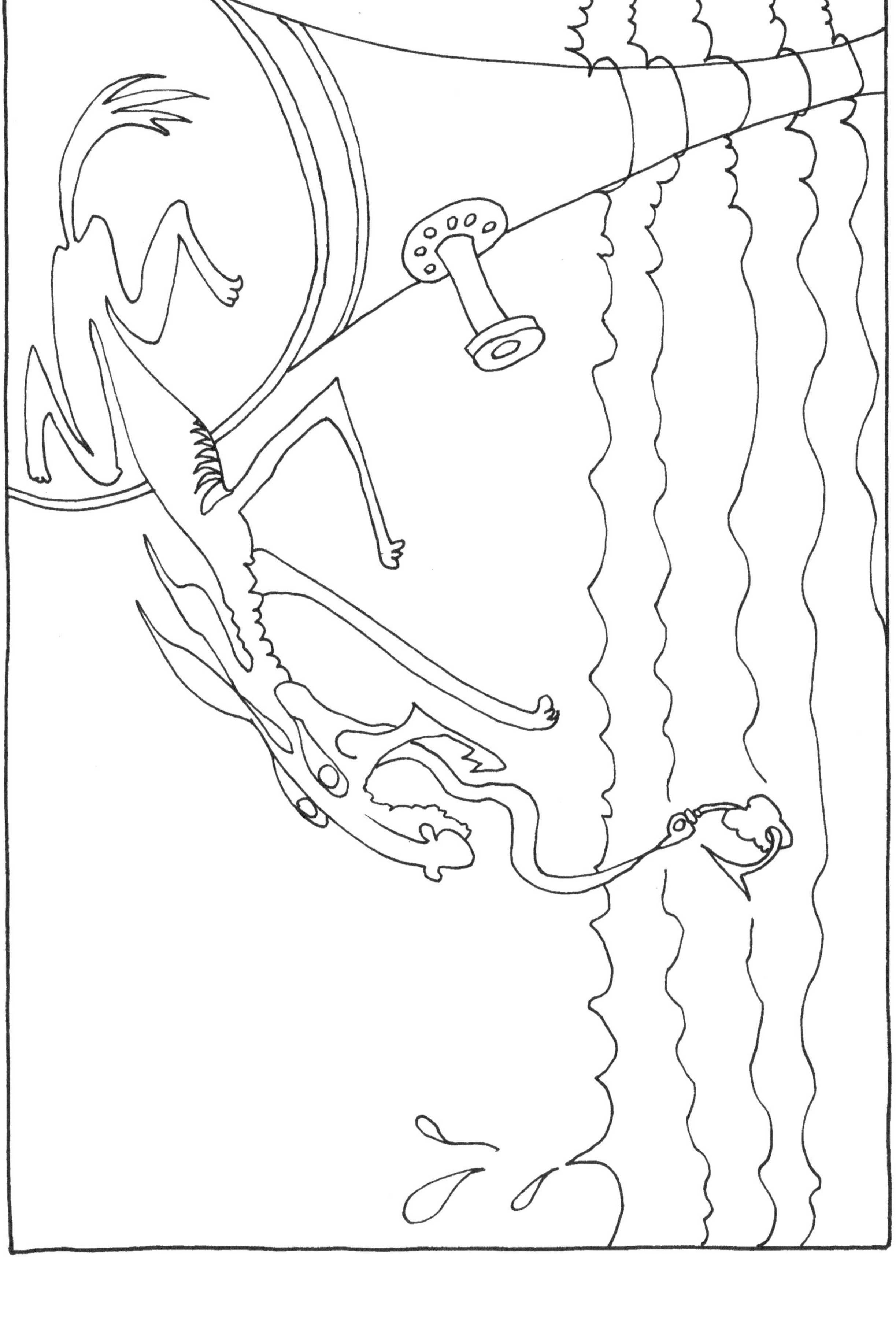

CREATURA #4

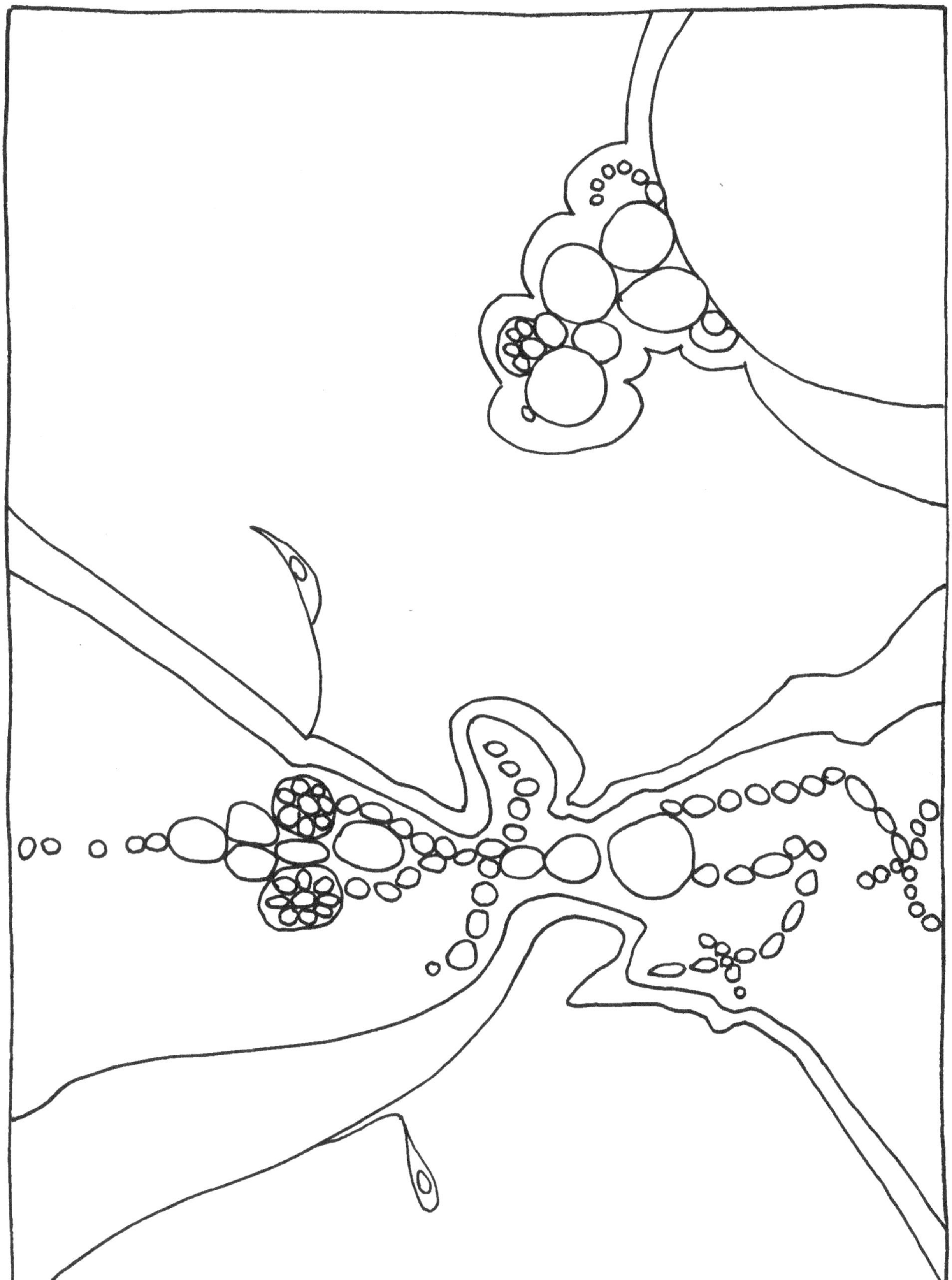

CREATURA #4

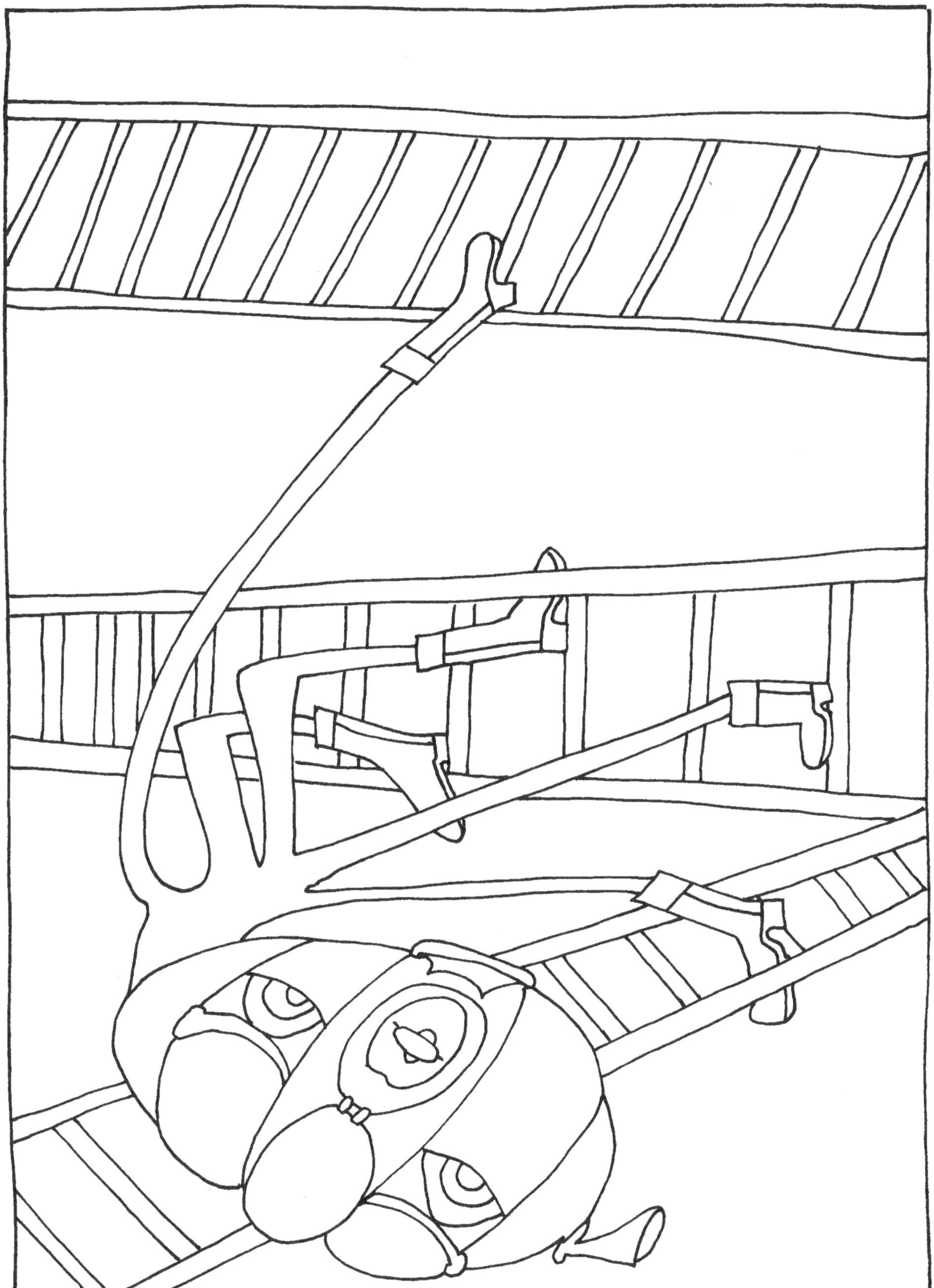

CREATURA #4 ©2018 Joan Worth

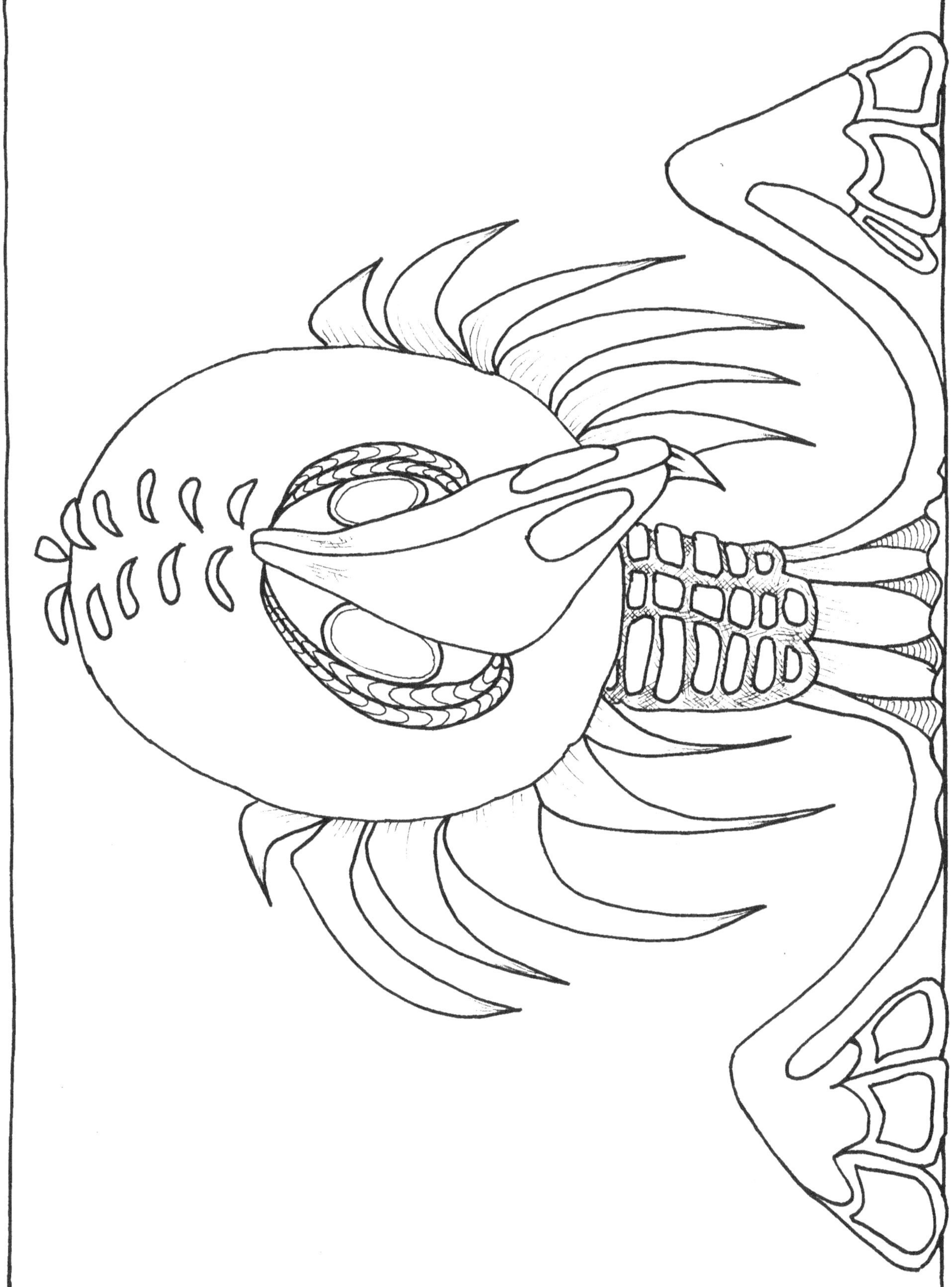

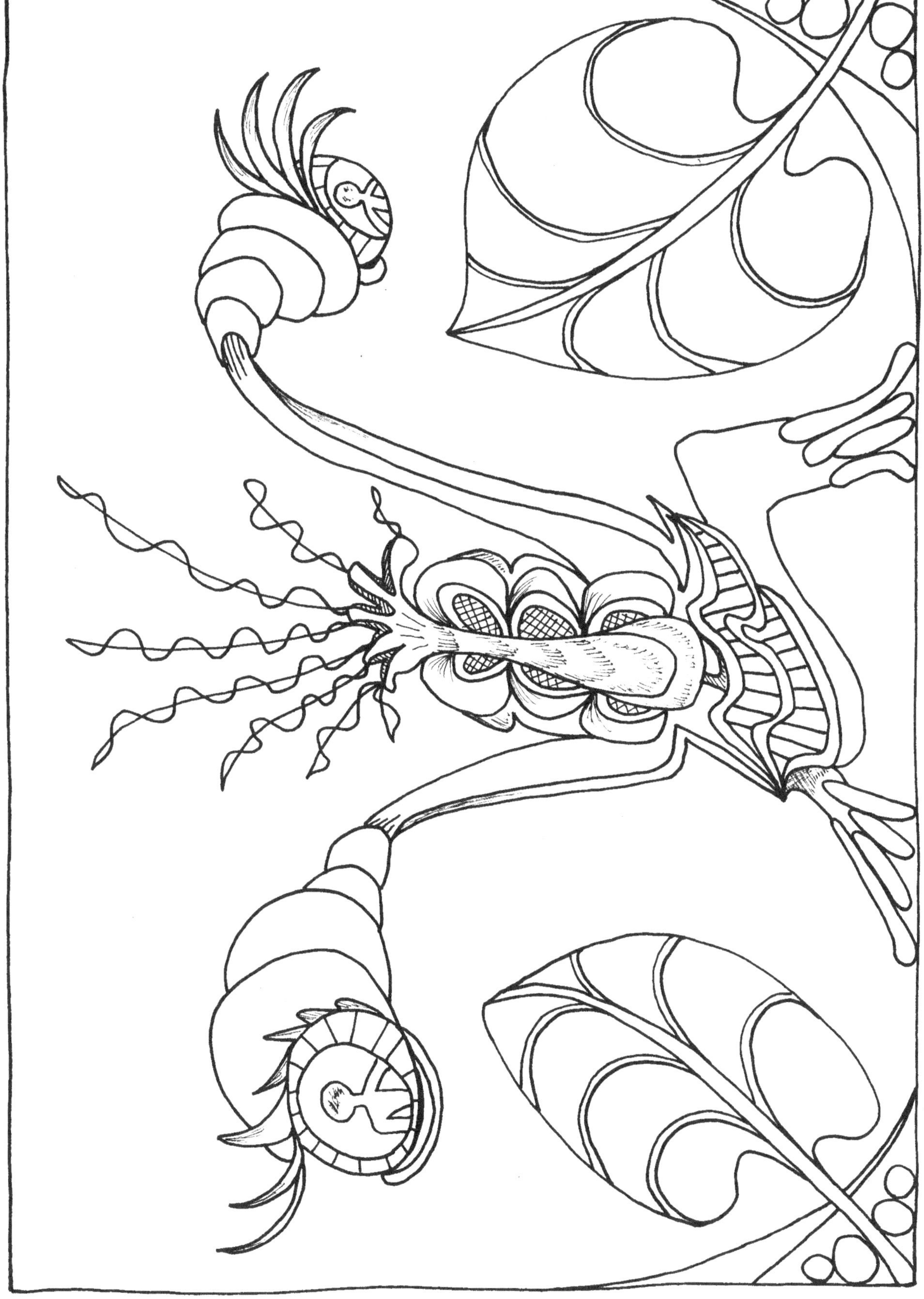

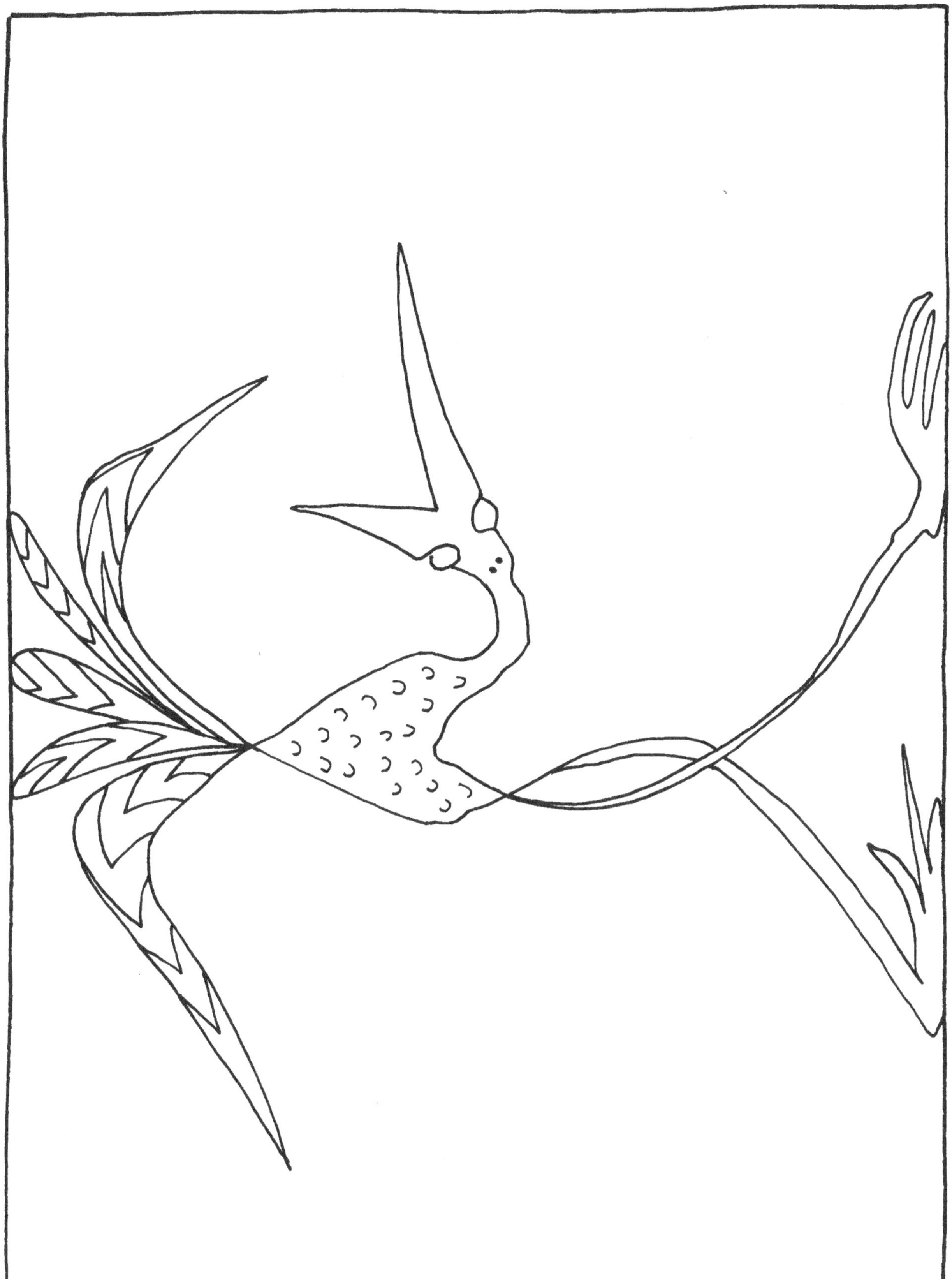

CREATURA #4 ©2018 Joan Worth

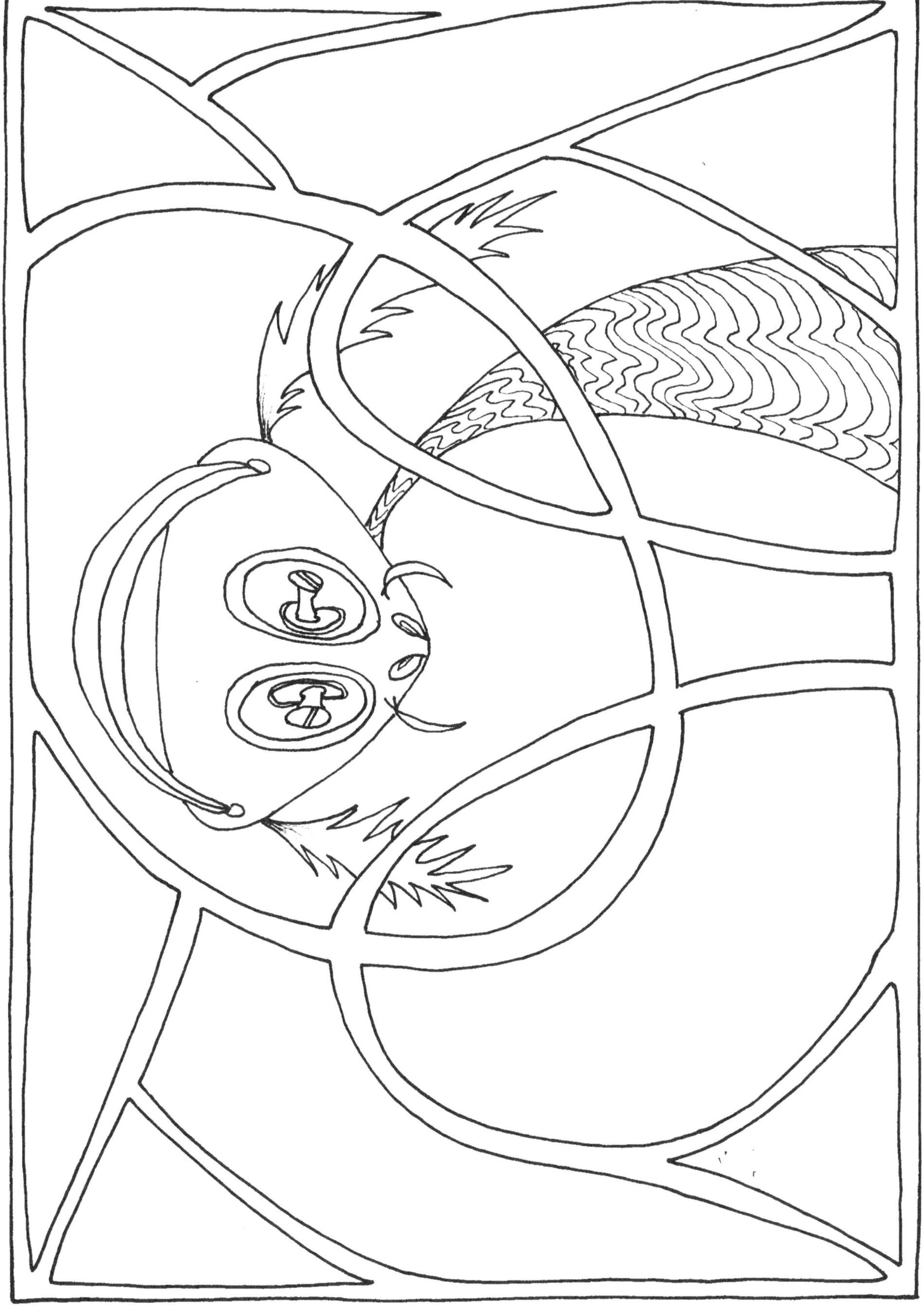

CREATURA #4 ©2018 Joan Worth

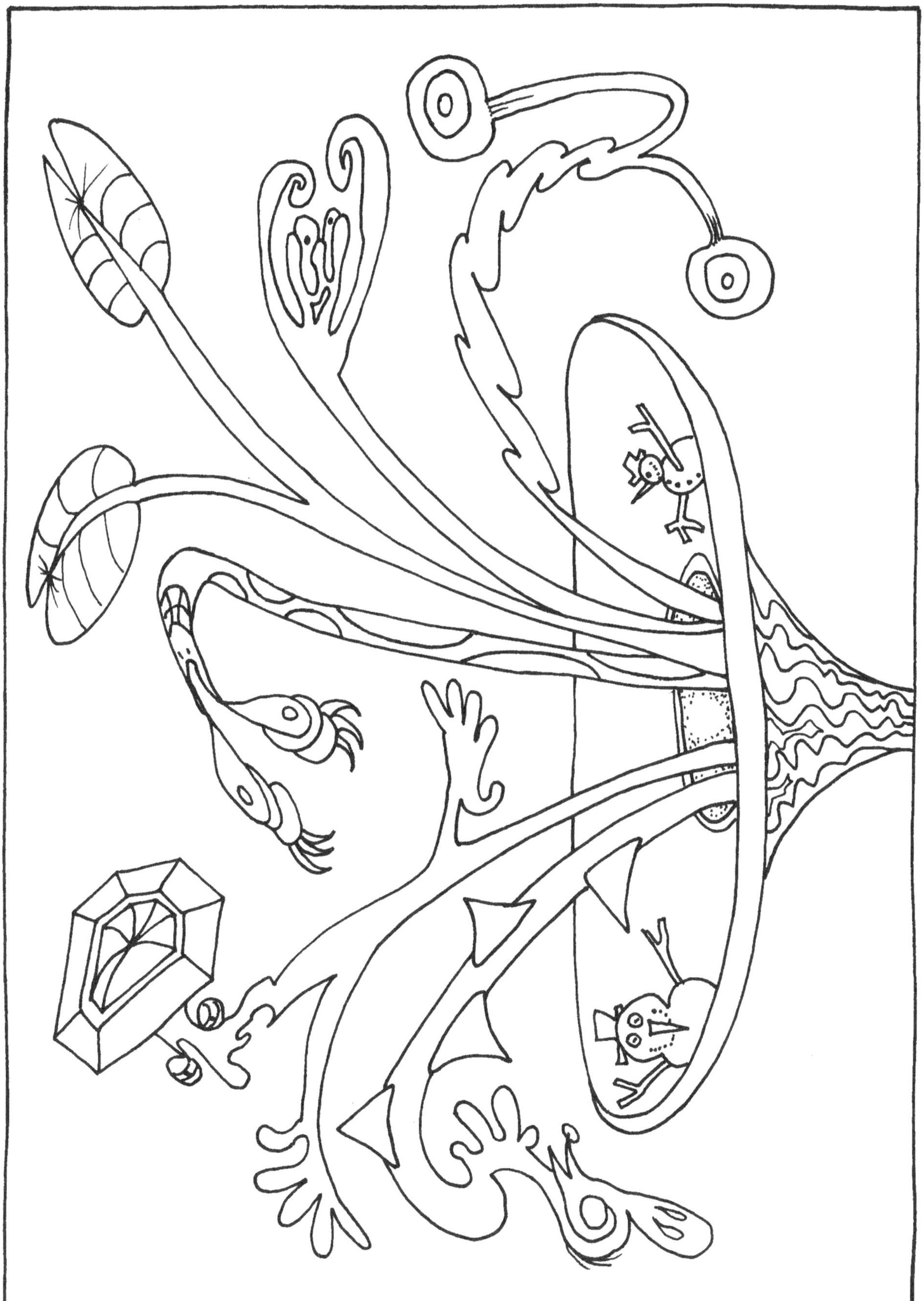

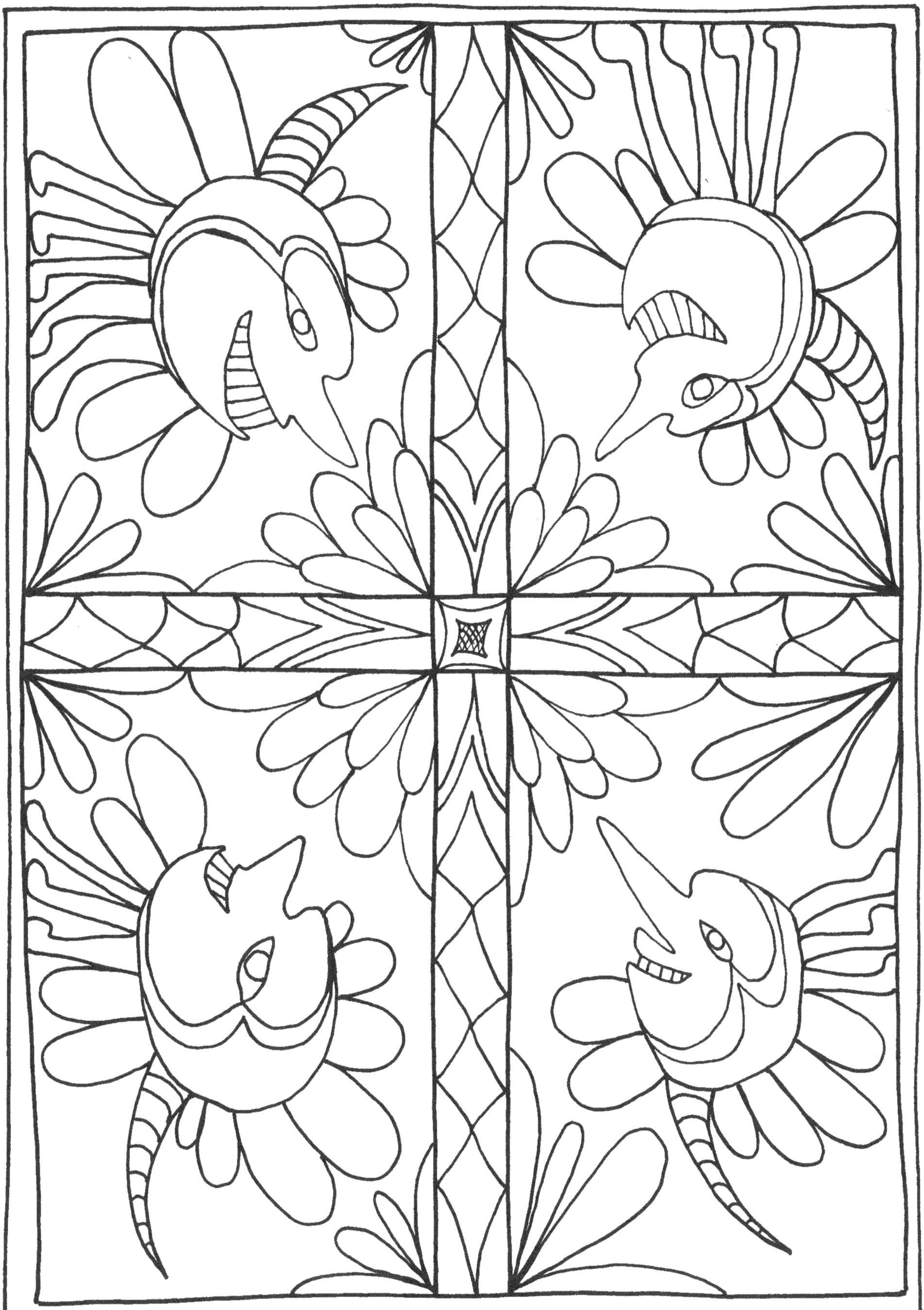

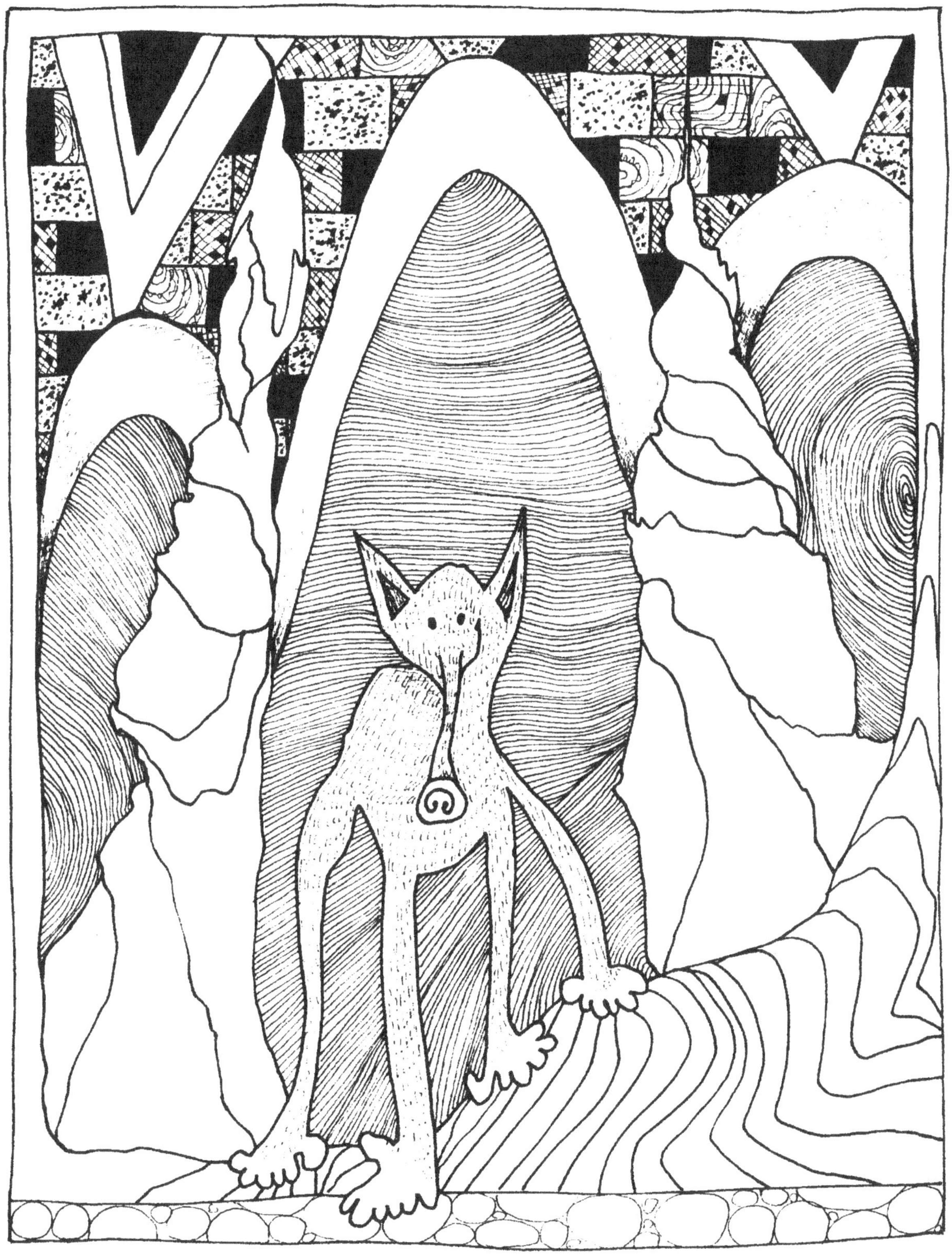

www.ingramcontent.com/pod-product-compliance
Lightning Source LLC
Chambersburg PA
CBHW081727220526
45468CB00008B/2000
9781984914170